The DRAMATIC EXPERIENCE
A guide to the reading of plays

By the same author

THE ELEMENTS OF DRAMA

THE DARK COMEDY

SHAKESPEARE'S STAGECRAFT

CHEKHOV IN PERFORMANCE

DRAMA, STAGE AND AUDIENCE

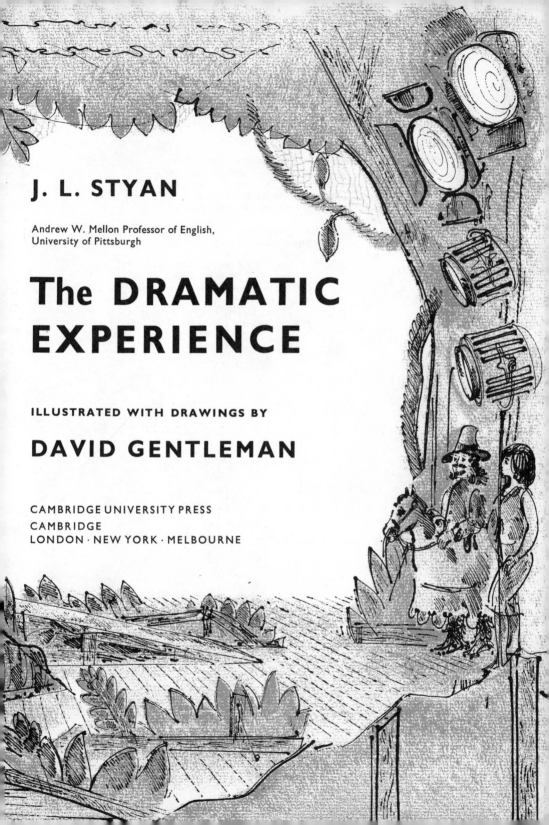

J. L. STYAN

Andrew W. Mellon Professor of English,
University of Pittsburgh

The DRAMATIC EXPERIENCE

ILLUSTRATED WITH DRAWINGS BY

DAVID GENTLEMAN

CAMBRIDGE UNIVERSITY PRESS
CAMBRIDGE
LONDON · NEW YORK · MELBOURNE

Published by the Syndics of the Cambridge University Press
The Pitt Building, Trumpington Street, Cambridge CB2 1RP
Bentley House, 200 Euston Road, London NW1 2DB
32 East 57th Street, New York, NY 10022, USA
296 Beaconsfield Parade, Middle Park, Melbourne 3206, Australia

hard covers ISBN: 0 521 06573 9
paperback ISBN: 0 521 09984 6

First published 1965
Reprinted 1971
First paperback edition 1975

Printed in Great Britain by
Jarrold and Sons Ltd, Norwich

TO L, D, K AND V

Contents

Preface

The purpose of this short book is to offer simple guidance to students faced with the cold text of a play and having no chance to act it themselves or to see it alive in the theatre. With its help, it is hoped that a few of the misconceptions which readily arise from the mere reading of drama will be avoided, and that a better understanding of the dramatist's intentions and a fuller enjoyment of the play will follow. The book aims, in effect, to make a contribution towards the stage-centred reform of drama teaching and appreciation.

As far as possible, reference in the text has been restricted to those plays most commonly met with in a study of English drama, especially those of Shakespeare; but the book is not intended as a substitute for the many useful commentaries available on English drama and the theatre, some of which are listed for further reading. It is written very much as a supplement to these, as a practical working aid to reading a play fully, a tool to keep to hand.

In writing the book I am much indebted to my wife, Brian Holbeche and Pat Roberts for sound advice and help, to Muriel Crane for valuable suggestions with the Reading Lists, and to Leonard Tibbitts from whose scholarly work on expression notation I borrowed my simplified version a number of years ago.

J. L. STYAN

UNIVERSITY OF HULL

Preface to the paperback edition

The issue of this edition suggests that the number of students is growing who think of a play, not as a book of words, but as a performance. Reading a play is not like reading a newspaper or a novel, and if we apply non-dramatic ideas to a play-text, like as not we will come to non-dramatic conclusions. We may enjoy unravelling a story or a character or a theme from the dialogue, but a play is not made of threads, nor does it work by ravelling them. It works by the simultaneous impact of all these elements and many more, constantly bombarding us, constantly changing.

It is deceptive because the text is written in words, superficially the same sort as are used for novels and insurance policies. But words in a play have merely the convenience of a code to be deciphered by the actors, and by an audience in a creative act of perception. The reader suffers the great handicap of working only from words on the page, when he must first perceive what they stand for.

In this edition I have tried to bring the book's modest reading lists up to date.

J. L. STYAN

UNIVERSITY OF PITTSBURGH

1   Seeing and hearing

A play is not like a novel or a poem

This is a truism that needs to be repeated. Because the playwright must put his ideas for his play into so many words on paper, it is all too easy to read them as if they work like those in other books. A composer of music writes a notation for the sounds in his mind, but the fullness of the music is heard only in performance; so it is with drama. Once one is in the habit of reading a play as if it were, say, a story that is all dialogue, or a poem that is broken up for speaking, then habits of thinking, useful for discussing a novel or a poem, can be applied wrongly to drama.

A moment's thought about a few of the differences between a novel and a play, and between a poem and a play, will put us on guard against some of the obvious mistakes.

A novel can pause in its career while its author draws attention to some detail he is anxious the reader should not miss, or while he gives his reader direct information about the thoughts of a character; a play on the other hand can only work through visible actors and what we can hear them say and see them do. Thus, by description, a novelist can, if he wishes, present a character virtually whole on his first page, but the playwright through his actor can give us only so much at a time; and for the most part he must *demonstrate* it. This accounts for the delightful immediacy of drama.

In some plays, of course, we may infer that a situation or a character is full and complete offstage, just as we know there is a great deal more of an iceberg beneath the surface. The good producer and actor, and the student too, test the quality of such a situation or character by exploring for what is not directly seen or heard. In the theatre an audience does this continuously, and this is one of the active pleasures of undergoing a play. Any detail the playwright wishes his audience to notice particularly, anything he wishes to 'tell' them, requires a special technique of 'signalling' into the auditorium. *These signals are being made all the time, and are the life of the play.*

A novel can move so freely and loosely in space and time that essentially space and time have not the same necessary importance as for the theatre; but physical space and actual time are the real and rigorous limitations of a play and its condition of working. Without them it could not be a play. An actor on his platform is alive in three dimensions, and, for however long he remains there, he must contribute also to our awareness of time, the fourth dimension. Furthermore, if great drama is achieved, these very limitations will have been turned into creative opportunities. The good playwright therefore practises his art with a strong sense of the economy the stage demands, making an ideal choice and arrangement of signals *imaginatively conceived in terms of particular space and time.*

A poem can convey its meaning to its reader even more directly than a novel. The poet selects and organizes words in patterns of sound, association and image; the reader for his part can linger his eye or his ear over the poem, reading it forwards and even backwards, making the pace of his reading exactly correspond with the needs of his own understanding, feeling and imagination. In a play, on the other hand, the good dramatist exactly controls the kind and intensity of our interest in the details of character and events on the stage. Moreover, he absolutely determines the sequence of the signals to the audience and always insists upon *a precise speed at which they are to be transmitted and received.*

The difference here is partly because the poet, like the novelist, thinks of his reader as an individual; the playwright must always think of an audience as a group. *Drama is a social activity; reading poetry is usually a private one.*

Of greatest importance is the fact that the poet can speak in his own voice, whereas the playwright must always translate his thoughts into terms of the theatre, splitting his mind into two or more minds, those of his characters, each with an individuality and life of his own. The poet speaks directly with the words, and these words are his poem; but the playwright's words are not his play. The playwright only speaks through his actors, who must in turn transform his words into signals of sight and sound to the spectators in the theatre. *Therefore the reader of a play must be ready to see and hear in his mind's eye and in his mind's ear.*

The essential differences may be summarized by diagrams, which are ones to return to regularly.

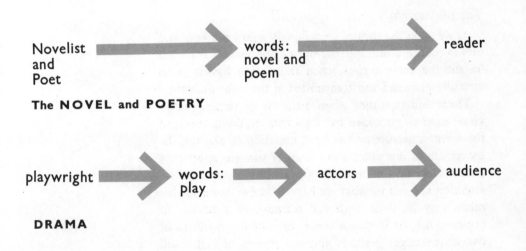

Novelist and Poet → words: novel and poem → reader

The NOVEL and POETRY

playwright → words: play → actors → audience

DRAMA

Lines of communication

3

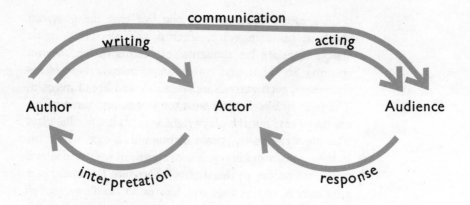

A theatre experience is circular

The actor interprets and the audience responds: everyone contributes to the performance

The playwright's system of signals

As we sit in the theatre we willingly adjust our eyes and ears to receive a multiple barrage of impressions from the instant the curtain rises, each impression having been carefully prepared and transmitted at the right moment.

There will be times when elements of mime, purely visual motions provided by the actor, are doing much of the work: a gesture or a sudden cessation of gesture, the movement of one actor away from or towards another, a pace upstage or a pace downstage, will hold our complete attention and tell us what we have to know. Some of this mime may be done with the restraint of a person in ordinary life, or it may assume some of the qualities of dance: the larger gestures and movements of ballet will often seem fitting when the style of the play is very different from everyday life. But in all plays, one character set against another, or two set against three, the single figure downstage or the significant separation of a group of characters upstage—such planning and composing of the stage picture must continuously change the image of the play the active spectator is creating within his mind.

There will be times when the actor's mask, or even his make-up, which after all is sometimes a form of mask, will illuminate the character the actor stands for. Perhaps his costume, its colour and its shape, will serve as a reminder of what he symbolizes, especially where it is set against, or is in harmony with, other costumes on the stage or the general décor of the scene. Perhaps the degree of brightness or shadow surrounding an actor will assist in forming or intensifying an impression. This is true also of the colour-tone of a scene, the colour of the lighting in conjunction with the colour of the décor and costuming.

For the most part, however, the voice of the actor, with all the great range of tone which the delicate human instrument can express, will be speaking to us: speech which ranges from the casual grunt and conversational idiom to the heightened artificiality of rhetorical poetry and lyrical song—operatic conventions are as permissible in a spoken play as in a musical play. A rush of speech, or a moment of complete silence, can make its point, just as can the introduction of music or other sound effects. And where there are two or more voices to be heard, we may expect a harmony or a counterpoint of tone and meaning to contribute to the play's richness.

The task of a reader is to feel *the cumulative impact of such impressions, controlled, like music, by a particular tempo.* These elements are mentioned, not only to suggest that drama is the most complicated of art forms, but also to remind us that many of them can be at work at the same time during a performance. Drama mixes the other arts with a fine disregard, calling at will upon ingredients which seem to belong to painting and sculpture, dance and music, poetry and the novel. We must be careful therefore not to think only of the last two in this astonishing list. Visual and aural, mimetic and verbal, all are facets of the one art of drama: reading the play, we dare not ignore this fact.

The next diagram invites you to piece out and then to juggle together those aspects of drama you can discover for yourself in the scene you are reading, and you will see that critics are justified in calling drama a truly composite art.

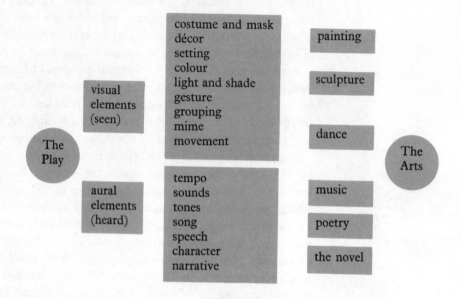

A way of looking at the ingredients of a play

Shakespeare's plays continually excite audiences because his own highly developed system of signals makes so many suggestions simultaneously. To take an example, *Macbeth* is an outstanding play if only because its signals are intense and full, and wholly capture our attention.

It is not easy to forget Macbeth on the point of going to King Duncan's room to murder him:

> wither'd murther,
> Alarum'd by his sentinel, the wolf,
> Whose howl's his watch, thus with his stealthy pace,
> With Tarquin's ravishing strides, towards his design
> Moves like a ghost. Thou sure and firm-set earth
> Hear not my steps, which way they walk . . .

Even in reading, the imagination is fired as the poetry vividly creates a living portrait of 'murther' and his wolf, both of whom the actor is in a sense enacting. Then in a flash of poetic association, the whole impression is transformed and reinforced by the mention of the loathsome Tarquinius who raped the virtuous Lucretia. By this the crime in Macbeth's mind is immediately measured on a particular scale of evil.

Yet read again, and we *hear* the whisper in Macbeth's voice sustained by a breathy hissing in the words; and we hear his screwed-up determination in the firm pressure of the metrical phrases. Listen again, and we *see* the crouch of the body, even the pain and ugliness in the face at 'wither'd murther'. Is there an alertness in the eyes at 'alarum'd'? Is there a gliding in the foot in the swing of the unstressed syllables which time Macbeth's steps? We *hear and see* the hush and pause on the throaty word 'ghost', and sense his hesitation as he turns to the audience in the pit on 'thou firm and sure-set earth', inviting our collaboration in his villainy, compelling us to enter into his experience.

Now, with the mind's eye, look again at the stage, that vast Elizabethan platform on which Macbeth is moving silently and alone. From the place close to us where he has just enacted the horror of killing, and impersonally evoked the atmosphere of brooding evil, he has a long journey to make to reach one of the upstage doors. This necessary progress of some forty feet (try this amazing distance for yourself) could have been for Shakespeare and his actor an embarrassment of space and time. But the dramatist uses this same distance, with its delay, to stretch our imagination, encouraging a powerful tension, while the lone actor's movement is given time to make murderers and victims of us all.

As good readers of drama we acquire the key to the 'code' each dramatist adopts for his actors. Read the lines aloud, get on your feet if need be, and you receive an immediate invitation to enter the dramatist's particular territory of make-believe: you begin to accept the experience as real when you know it is unreal. We try to receive the *theatre experience* each dramatist offers, and this does not turn solely on the presence of a playhouse, a full-scale set and skilled actors, but on the intimate experience peculiar to dramatizing. This is one that is neither pretending, nor quite being. It is an experience in which part of oneself is surrendered that one may take a new shape born of the active imagination, a critical time when the human faculty of sharing the minds and feelings of others is wholly alive. However unpolished, the play becomes a physical and four-dimensional thing, and its language acquires the refreshing property of being *felt*.

Perhaps only a highly poetic language like that in *Macbeth* can provide a complete code for the actor and the audience?—poetry being as precise and concentrated a choice and arrangement of words as possible. Nevertheless, every playwright, whatever his playhouse and of whatever kind his play, must imply some such system, although of course he may not always be good at using it. Let us see what Congreve and Shaw do in Restoration and modern times. They are writing in prose, and quite colloquial prose too; but it is dramatic prose and it brings the stage alive.

Congreve writes for horizontal playing, with his actors in a line facing the audience like the figures in a sculptural frieze, not acting in depth as we find in Shakespeare; but the sense of direct contact with his audience is still very strong. Here is how the scintillating Millamant finally accepts Mirabell's famous proposal of marriage in *The Way of the World*. Mirabell is onstage, but she talks to Mistress Fainall, who serves as her confidante in this episode:

MILLAMANT. Fainall, what shall I do? Shall I have him? I think I must have him.

MRS FAINALL. Ay, ay, take him, take him, what shou'd you do?

MILLAMANT. Well then—I'll take my death I'm in a horrid fright—Fainall, I shall never say it—Well—I think—I'll endure you.

MRS FAINALL. Fy, fy, have him, have him, and tell him so in plain terms: for I am sure you have a mind to him.

MILLAMANT. Are you? I think I have—and the horrid man looks as if he thought so too—Well, you ridiculous thing you, I'll have you. . . .

This really does have to be spoken aloud, indeed mimed, before its full meaning is felt; and in this it has its own kind of poetry.

We cannot help noticing first that Millamant's lines are unmistakably written for an actress with arms and legs and a fan and the delightfully free and dancing costume of the period. In contrast with Mistress Fainall's insistent repetitions, 'take him, take him . . . have him, have him', which betoken a simple gesture from left or right of the stage and unchanging throughout the passage, Millamant's lines suggest many, many delicate movements of her head and neck, of her arms and fan, even to the point where she prods her lover in the ribs with it. Voice and body are one. We must see too that she stands centre-stage between Fainall and Mirabell, so that all her motions sway between these two, from side to side, retreating and advancing, motions not unlike those of a dancer.

There is another quality in this dialogue we should not miss. The curious arrangement of the sense apparently suggests that she is talking to Fainall for most of the time, but in point of fact her remarks are really thrown over her fan, working as it is at full flourish, to Mirabell: 'Shall I have him? I think I must have him.'

Yet again, a question intended for Mirabell like the 'Shall I have him?' is even more certainly addressed to the spectators at her feet, who indeed probably made an enthusiastic answer, for the interest in the outcome of Mirabell's proposal reaches a peak of excitement at this point. And remarks like 'I'll take my death I'm in a horrid fright' and 'the horrid man looks as if he thought so too' are unquestionably for the audience. How can we be sure? Because the irony of the whole piece rests upon our certain knowledge that Millamant is very much the mistress of the situation, that she is obviously in no fright at all, and that she can tease poor Mirabell to her heart's content. We know that her remarks are a little joke with the audience at the expense of her wretched suitor's feelings (that is, if *he* does not know it to be a joke too), and perhaps at the expense of all would-be bridegrooms.

This analysis may suggest some of the fun to be seen and heard in the dialogue; but has such a scene any *meaning?* It is indeed alive with dramatic meaning because it epitomizes one aspect of the commonest of sex relationships, the courtship, one in which, says Congreve, the fair sex finally holds all the cards. In another writer this scene could have been a tragedy for the man, and it is for Alceste in Molière's comedy of *The Misanthrope*. In *The Way of the World* Congreve makes his points in a delightfully witty manner: they are light, but not necessarily therefore *slight*.

Such freedom of movement, such by-play of comment and aside with the audience, such insistent invitations to see and hear and be involved, are not readily found in more modern drama. The nineteenth-century playwright saw his play set back and framed between the two pillars of the proscenium arch, and his audience was invited to watch people from another world living in another room. Thus there is some justice in wondering whether the loss of contact with the spectator may not have destroyed his true participation in the play. Yet, however secluded his stage, the dramatist in any age who has a sense of the theatre may still use our faculties of sight and hearing to draw us into the play.

The actress playing the Maid in Shaw's *Saint Joan* has a striking first entrance. Robert de Baudricourt, Joan's pompous squire, is sitting at his table 'magisterially' We have just seen him wielding his petty power over his servant, and we are waiting to see what form his temper will take when he is confronted by an impudent peasant girl. We are also curious to see her recoil from a fearsome exterior like his. However, whatever we anticipate, this is likely to be different from the brisk and businesslike girl we are shown and from the scene that follows. We are taken by storm, as Robert is:

JOAN (*bobbing a curtsy*). Good morning, captain squire. Captain: you are to give me a horse and armour and some soldiers, and send me to the Dauphin. Those are your orders from my Lord.

Even in reading it is hard to mistake the breathlessness of her long sentence with its 'and . . . and . . . and'. Its speech-music has a thrust and finality. That same breathlessness must indicate how impatiently she bursts into the presence of this little tyrant, how curt is the gesture of the curtsy. The measured authority of her final sentence, and

the vigorous contrast between '*your* orders' and '*my* Lord', not only put Robert firmly in his place, but triumphantly assert Joan's allegiance at the same time. Robert, who asks to be deflated well enough, must gasp in the audible silence that follows her demands.

The by-play with the audience is not felt through the direct address of Shakespeare and Congreve, but it is equally there, and the stage is equally alive. First, the visual shock of an exciting entrance into the setting of the picture-frame (the 'strong entrance') is fully employed; more importantly, Joan's manner is an extreme and calculated contrast to that of the frightened Steward a moment before. This is possible because Shaw is fully alert to the contribution to the drama the spectator is willing to make.

There is more to be said later about the methods by which these three different kinds of theatre set to work on the audience, but for the moment it is fair to say that these signs for movement and speech, stillness and silence, mood and tone, are not only the playwright's means of reaching the spectator through his actors, but at the same time *his means of realizing his dramatic idea.*

A play must be particular

For we have been talking in another way about the process of composing a play, observing the discussion the writer has with himself as he fingers his pen. Many factors govern his decisions whether to put more or less emphasis on what is heard than on what is seen, to write in verse or in prose, to present his subject in terms of tragedy or of comedy, to accelerate or decelerate the tempo of his scene, and so on for all manner of vital technical considerations. The chief of these factors may be the tradition of his theatre and the customary expectations of his audience, but at all stages of composition the dramatist must be busy deciding how he may transform his ideas into relevantly dramatic sights and sounds, ones which will communicate his point to the spectator as efficiently as possible.

The playwright's theatre practice must be an exact and economical business: what is called the 'action' on the stage is the careful particularizing in specifically human terms of what he wants to say. King Lear's understanding of the world of God and man must be represented in his *specific* relationships with other people—with two bad daughters and a good one; he reaches the crisis of his thinking in the *specific* challenge to the storm; his humility is marked by the *specific* gesture of stripping off his clothes and linking arms with a mad beggar. Such particularities guide us towards an understanding of the play's theme and meaning.

In another century the Irishman J. M. Synge conveys his bitter sense of the nobility of human life by presenting on the stage an Irish fisherwife. In *Riders to the Sea* we are taken into a particular cottage on the west coast of Ireland; we see how Maurya, the mother of a sea-going family, lives her narrow life; we see her lose first one, then the other, of her remaining sons; and we hear how she accepts her lot. Notice how in this remote little tragedy Maurya's last words speak to us in very particular, and yet far-reaching, terms:

Michael has a clean burial in the far north, by the grace of the Almighty God. Bartley will have a fine coffin out of the white boards, and a deep grave surely. What more can we want than that? No man at all can be living for ever, and we must be satisfied.

Only because of this insistent stress on the particular, on what we can see and hear, does drama aspire to the universal, and this quality it shares with other literary forms.

There is some danger that the dramatist may under-estimate or over-estimate the importance of particularity. On the one hand, the medieval *Everyman*, like many modern expressionist plays, constantly risks losing all humanity in aiming at the universal, risks seeming as abstract as an algebraic equation. However, *Everyman* short-circuits much of the need for particularity because its central figure retains enough natural sensibility to make the play a living thing. On the other hand, *Riders to the Sea*, like many modern plays in naturalistic settings, risks being over-particular in the isolation of its setting and in its choice of fishermen and their wives to demonstrate the suffering of mankind. If the play does not make us feel like Maurya, there is a chance that we shall dismiss it as irrelevant to our own lives.

In the true magic of the theatre, which has nothing at all to do with the sales-talk of bright lights and enchanted evenings, the good dramatist perfectly crystallizes his thoughts and feelings, and at the same time grants his audience some common material of human life for recognition and understanding, for the exercise of that unique faculty of sharing the experience of others. His words must provide a precise framework for what we are to see and hear, and this dramatic precision is what makes for 'good theatre'. It may or may not be easy to read, but it will certainly be alive in the theatre. In the last analysis, its quality is to be measured by the only test—performance in the theatre, and when we read a play critically, we are first and foremost making this test of stageworthiness in our imagination.

2   The stage alive

The playwright and theatre practice

Any play depends to an important degree upon the people for whom it is written and their reason for going to the theatre; and the way the play is written for acting and speaking depends upon the theatre in which it is to be performed. These two factors of audience and playhouse are not really separable of course, and much of the fascination in the study of drama comes from the imaginative excitement of deducing the relative contributions of the 'why' and the 'how' of the theatre, the relation between the written text, the audience and the play's means of presentation.

The congregation in a church and the audience in a cinema may both be a mixture of all sorts of people, but their purpose in meeting together in a church for worship and in a cinema for entertainment affects everything. Since in church it is important to know what to expect, the service takes a ritual and repeated form; in a cinema it is just as important *not* to be able to anticipate the pattern of the ceremony. In a church, the building is so arranged and lit that there is every inducement to participate in the service; in a cinema we sit in darkness and submit to the illusion of the bright screen.

Even considered in isolation, the architecture of a playhouse can tell a good deal about the play, the attitudes and purposes of its audience, as well as the kind of acting and performance. It is of special value and interest to the reader of a play to know the size and shape of its original theatre, since this points directly to *the particular theatre experience it offered.*

15

The Greek theatre

The relation of stage and audience: in the Greek theatre

The ancient Greek theatre had to be able to hold at least the whole male and free population of the city-state whose religious festival it housed. To have built such a playhouse with a roof would have been quite impossible, and so the Greeks chose natural, open-air sites on conveniently shaped hill-sides, and arranged the auditorium as nearly like a bowl as possible in order that all should see and hear. The huge London Palladium today seats 2,388 people; it therefore staggers the imagination to learn that in Greece the restored Theatre of Epidaurus seats 20,000 (and has perfect acoustics), and that in classical times the Theatre of Ephesus actually held as many as 56,000. This single factor of immense size dominates everything in the presentation of Greek drama; and this same factor makes it very difficult to present it satisfactorily in any modern medium which requires that it be scaled down: thus, television and Greek tragedy are a contradiction in terms.

Such dimensions did not permit the naturalistic drama familiar in modern times. The distance of the farthest member of the audience from the actors was such that words and tones of conversation were not to be expected. Subtle gestures, too, were useless, and certainly the wrinkle of the eye or the pursing of lips seen in the close-up of cinema and television were out of the question. The acting had to be bold, and perhaps a little like the mimed movement of a ballet in slow motion. Gesture, chiefly of the arms, was broad, and the words rhetorical and nearer to song than speech. An important character wore raised boots, a tall head-dress and a long costume to increase his stature (this was padded to preserve normal proportions), and much of his character was fixed from the start by the mask and symbolic costume he wore.

It follows that what at first glance seems to be dialogue in Greek tragedy is in fact a series of speeches alternating between two or three voices made to echo, contrast with, or otherwise illuminate one another. Or else it is choric song which provides an emphatic commentary on the story, rather than action in the modern sense. The detail of real life is not found even in the more domestic Euripides: at a pathetic moment in *The Trojan Women*, for example, when Andromache learns that her young son is to be brutally killed, she remains a very stylized mother indeed (her part was originally, of course, played by a man): she clasps her ill-fated son to her, but she must explain *in so many words* that the boy is weeping, throwing his arms around her neck and kissing her.

Greek drama, with its chorus of commentators at its heart, is thus a most formal art and a massive one by any modern standards, but nevertheless the unique shape of its theatre suggests that the audience felt itself to be participating in the ceremony. This interesting contradiction expresses itself in the speeches, most of which were a direct address to the audience of powerful urgency. Above all, the familiarity of the audience with the subjects of the plays, which were the heroic myths and legends they all knew from childhood, and with the ritual form of their presentation, which did not change from year to year, made what might read like a cold drama into a warm and impressive experience shared between the actors and the spectators.

In medieval drama

Because of its 'theatre' the other great religious drama of the western world, the drama of the medieval miracle and mystery plays, embodies another extraordinary contradiction between content and style, one of a very different order. No drama has been played in conditions of such intimacy, and yet been required to be so distant.

The audience at the drama festivals of medieval times included everyone. All good Christians (and, because of the spirit of holiday, probably not such good ones, to judge from the proclamations read to the people before performance) came into town to see the stories of the Bible enacted by their friends in the many craft guilds of the time. Again it had to be an open-air theatre, but this time

The Medieval theatre

the stage was broken up into a series of platforms or 'mansions' set about a town square, or else the actors toured the streets from point to point on elaborately decorated carts or 'pageants'. A drama played in this way had to be episodic; it may seem to us now to be a large number of short one-act plays loosely strung together by the Bible theme.

A greater subject than the progress of man from the Creation to the Last Judgment is difficult to conceive, yet because of the intimacy of playing from a cart in a street or a square, medieval drama lost much of the formal quality of the Greek. It came to be a drama of extra-ordinary contrasts, of cruelty and comedy, and of poetic dignity and homely simplicity. The cramped towns with their narrow streets would have been crowded with people standing shoulder to shoulder and packed at upstairs win-dows, probably surrounding the pageant and its acting area. In consequence, the surviving texts suggest a strange mixture of acting styles. They range from the ritualistic manner suitable for a religious drama and probably borrowed from the Church, to a most incongruously colloquial repartee.

Where strict adherence to the Bible stories was not necessary, our less sophisticated ancestors took every opportunity to introduce common and realistic life. Intimacy affects the nature of a play at its roots. We shall never know how the beautiful story of the three shepherds came at Wakefield to be a story of *four* shepherds, the extra one being a comic rascal. We shall never know how Noah came to acquire a wife at Chester, though we can guess that when one of the all-male cast assumed skirts, the quarrel between a brazen Mrs Noah and her reverent old husband became, year after year, a high point of the performance.

The Greek and medieval theatres provide useful comparisons, but we shall be concerned after this with the types of English drama we are most likely to meet: Elizabethan, Restoration, Eighteenth Century and Modern.

In the Elizabethan theatre

In the Elizabethan theatre the wide audience in close intimacy with the actor remained, while the playwright was relieved of his religious responsibilities, and the function of his acting company became more professional and commercial. But the tradition of medieval drama had prepared the ground for England's greatest experiment in the art of the theatre. The Elizabethan theatre and what it could do for the writer and the actor must therefore be at the centre of our studies. However, although we may enjoy a play by Shakespeare in London or at Stratford-upon-Avon today, and the play may achieve great success with the public, can we be sure it was the same kind of success in its original conditions of playing, the same kind of dramatic experience?

A study of what we imagine the Globe theatre to have been is the key to our understanding of Shakespeare the playwright and craftsman, inexhaustibly trying new ways of exploiting his stage. We talk of the 'conventions' of his theatre, but this is not just a matter of knowing that Shakespeare's women were played by boys (though this certainly throws light on his handling of love scenes), nor of accepting the strange inability of one character to recognize another in disguise (Edgar as a beggar is unknown to his own father), nor of accepting their abrupt way of falling in and out of love in the comedies (witness the odd behaviour of Olivia and Orsino in *Twelfth Night*).

No, the Elizabethan convention implies a use of the stage which is written into every word of speech and gesture. It is part of the imaginative experience for both actor and audience, making the excitement of Iago's aside to Othello when they see Desdemona with Cassio, 'Hah! I like not that', an excitement of intense and emphatic audience participation. It encourages the dramatist to chop freely between pathetic and comic, noble and ignoble scenes, between quiet and noisy ones, creating the strangely mixed flavour of romantic comedy in *Twelfth Night* or of farcical tragedy in *Troilus and Cressida*. It explains why a long soliloquy of Hamlet's does not in fact stop the play dead, but creates a high point of dramatic pressure on the sensibilities of the audience. The very spirit in the auditorium is affected by 'convention'.

Although all the details of the Globe may never be certainly known, we have enough of its elements to bring it alive in our imagination. It is known:

1. That the spectators, over 2,000 of them, swarmed *round three sides* at least of the stage.
2. That the play was *acted in daylight*, without the modern illusions of stage setting and lighting, and with a *minimum of scenery* and properties.
3. That the chief acting area, with access from two upstage doors, was *a very large open platform*, estimated at over 40 feet wide and nearly 30 feet deep. These dimensions provided a primary playing space larger than any existing in London today.
4. That the rear façade of the platform was *a permanent architectural and therefore neutral 'set'*, providing two or three levels and many acting areas.

It is easy to contrast the dramatist's limited opportunities on the modern picture-frame stage, which is flat, tapering and two-dimensional, and contains but one level

The Elizabethan theatre

Free sight-lines.

Actor advances
    to the hub of the wheel.

Downstage position dominant.

Restricted sight-lines.

Actor withdraws
    into the picture frame.

Upstage position dominant.

To illustrate essential differences between the Elizabethan and Modern stages

and one acting space. If today some special structure is built on the stage serving as a second level to provide visual contrast and variety, it eats the acting space, and indeed may have to be moved off every time it lends spurious significance to a scene which does not call for it. Ours tends to be a stage of visual monotony, and this has to be overcome in other ways.

What sort of drama would one therefore expect to see on the bare, but spacious and varied, stage of the Globe? First, a drama which places a remarkable emphasis on the actor; both on his voice and his words, and on what meaning he can create with his body, its gesture and movement. Secondly, a drama which involves the spectator not only by his physical nearness to the stage, but also by what is demanded of him through an active imagination. A drama, finally, which offers the playwright an imaginative freedom in space and time, an unprecedented opportunity to juxtapose scene with scene in striking and incongruous arrangements of place and mood, and to create a rhythm in his action controlling the very life of the play.

All these qualities are nevertheless indivisible, because the open stage of the Globe above all encouraged the dramatist to write a poetic drama, one with the vitality and the unity of a living and growing thing.

Editors of *Macbeth* write the stage direction 'a heath' to remind the reader of the setting for the witches: but on the naked platform they could never be anywhere else. Nor are we likely to suppose that Lady Macbeth reads the letter from her husband on the heath. When we see an actor dressed as a soldier patrolling the front of the platform and clasping his arms as if he were cold, and when in a strained tone he calls up the long diagonal distance to the upstage door, 'Who's there?', we have no need to be told that he is on guard on the battlements of Hamlet's castle, or that it is a cold and misty night. When in *Antony and Cleopatra* the Queen enters, we are straight away in the imaginary world of Egypt; when we see Octavia, we are back in Rome. It is thus the actor, prompted by the suggestions in the words, who shifts the centre of interest even within a scene, and who provides the momentum of the play in more ways than as a character in a plot; as in a radio play, the listener is willing to be nimble of mind, leaping great distances or accepting a complete change of atmosphere at the suggestion of a sound or a voice. In Shakespeare, the excitement of battle is not in shifting from 'one part of the field' to 'another part of the field', but always in sensing the sway of fortune in the fight: the interest lies in human behaviour, and not in military tactics.

It is curiously true that if the place is sufficiently localized, the time of the day or the time of the year

becomes fixed too, as if on a stage set as a drawing-room
with a mantelpiece, the mantelpiece demands a clock. We
begin to ask of a naturalistic scene, when are they going to
eat next? What time do they go to bed? The eye flies to
the programme to discover whether it is 'later that
evening' or 'two months afterwards'. In the Elizabethan
theatre, time, like space, exists only for the drama of the
play. It places a pressure on the spectator or relaxes it,
urging a rhythm on the play which in turn puts weight on
certain sequences of the action. So a quiet Desdemona
sings and prepares for sleep, while we impatiently await
the terrible return of Othello. Or in *Julius Caesar*, we do
not drowse with the servants as we listen to the 'sleepy
tune' on the eve of the momentous civil war: we remain
alert with Brutus. Some scenes will throb in the mind,
others in contrast will remain cool and thoughtful. When
we refer to a play's style we should not perhaps think first
of its poetic imagery, or of its high or low life, but of its
special quality of rhythm.

Shakespeare only refers to time when he wants us to
remember it: as when the night passes in *A Midsummer
Night's Dream*, or when the bell tolls and Macduff knocks
on the castle door on the night of Duncan's murder, or
when Edmund is suddenly reminded that he has given
the order to hang Lear and Cordelia.

The Elizabethan play has no scene-divisions, and
Shakespeare wrote only long 'one-act' plays. His free,
flexible stage encouraged rapid changes of scene. How
easily the platform fills for the street-fight at the opening
of *Romeo and Juliet*, the emotional excitement rising as the
visual picture multiplies—and how easily Shakespeare can
clear the stage and change the mood again, leaving a rueful
and solitary Romeo with his friend Benvolio:

> BENVOLIO. Good morrow, cousin.
> ROMEO. Is the day so young?

At a stroke we are out of the public world of civil dissen-
sion and into the private mind of a lovesick youth. Against
the dangerous gaiety of Capulet's ball, idyllic love is
matched with the tension of Tybalt's growing fury. The

mixture of incongruous scenes increases until Romeo is banished and the Prince again addresses a full stage, thus:

> let Romeo hence in haste,
> Else when he's found, that hour is his last.

But almost before the stage has cleared, Juliet appears on the terrace and calls for her lover in pathetic ignorance of what has happened:

> Gallop apace, you fiery-footed steeds . . .

The results of compounding the ingredients like this are perhaps felt only in the theatre.

Shakespeare never forgets the space between actor and
actor and between actor and spectator. On every occasion
when we read 'Look where he comes', a gesture-comment
he often uses, it should remind us of the deep stage and of
the need to draw the spectator's attention to an important
entrance. Thus two hard-bitten Roman soldiers introduce
Antony and Cleopatra for a first impression:

> Look where they come:
> Take but good note, and you shall see in him
> The triple pillar of the world transform'd
> Into a strumpet's fool. Behold and see.

So we learn what the army thinks: is there a more ridiculous figure than the fool of a strumpet? And since
Demetrius and Philo speak for us downstage and into our
private ear, we do indeed look. But what do we hear?

CLEOPATRA. If it be love indeed, tell me how much.
ANTONY. There's beggary in the love that can be reckon'd.
CLEOPATRA. I'll set a bourn how far to be belov'd.
ANTONY. Then must thou needs find out new Heaven, new
  Earth.

So we judge for ourselves.

Downstage on the Elizabethan platform is a kind of

Antony and Cleopatra, I, i.

Antony
Cleopatra

Demetrius
Philo

As You Like It, I, ii,

Celia
Rosalind
Orlando

Movement in depth on the Elizabethan stage

no-man's-land, a neutral area where the actor can get into immediate touch with the spectator, and where the spectator takes him at face-value. Upstage the actor remains detached, often an object for criticism by the spectator, who is always in a sense 'downstage'. Thus, in a different pattern, we watch with amusement as poor Rosalind of *As You Like It* falls in love with Orlando, stammering and uncertain what to do. Meanwhile an embarrassed Celia pulls her towards the upstage door, and an entranced Orlando opens his heart. This is the scene:

ROSALIND. He calls us back: my pride fell with my fortunes,
    I'll ask him what he would: did you call sir?
    Sir, you have wrestled well, and overthrown
    More than your enemies.
CELIA. Will you go coz?
ROSALIND. Have with you: fare you well (*Exeunt*).
ORLANDO. What passion hangs these weights upon my tongue?
    I cannot speak to her, yet she urg'd conference.

Distinctions between contrasted characters, between Rosalind and Phoebe, between Cordelia and her sisters, between Malcolm and Macbeth, between Hamlet and Claudius, between Hal and Falstaff, and many others, are made implicitly by their relative placing on the stage in relation to the spectator.

Elizabethan drama, for all the wonders of its poetry, is therefore by no means lacking in visual excitement: its stage invited striking visual patterns and contrasts. It was a stage alive at one time with a lone figure on the vast space after a crowded scene (Hal and his 'I know you all' after the riotous tavern scene, Hamlet and his 'O that this too too solid flesh' after the pompous ceremonial of the court, Henry V in camp on the night before the battle of Agincourt); or alive at another time with a duologue designed to make the audience respond by what it sees of behaviour as well as by what it hears (Brutus and Cassius in their tent, Ross breaking the news of Lady Macduff's murder, Iago taunting Othello, Rosalind teasing Orlando, Titania caressing Bottom). The Globe invited a very varied dramatic technique because a firm relationship existed between its stage and the spectator.

29

In Restoration times

In the theatre of the Restoration and the eighteenth century (different as these were in style), the actor did not lose touch with his smaller audience of upper-class people. Yet it was a transitional theatre (as indeed all theatres must be, since drama is always changing as society is changing), and in it we can see the modern picture-frame stage at its birth. Moreover, we can feel the clash between the old and the new in the dramatic experience offered by the plays written for it.

It is a smaller, indoor theatre: Sir Christopher Wren's design for Drury Lane in 1674 suggests a capacity of less than 500, and there are only 36 feet from the stage to the back row. The proscenium arch appears, creating a space behind it which demanded to be filled with wings and back shutters, that is, scenery which is painting a picture. Not that this made for scenic illusion in the modern sense— curtains were not used between acts until late in the eighteenth century, properties for the use of the actors were changed in sight of the audience, and the setting was itself so rigidly symmetrical and unreal that there was almost nothing of pretence about it. Furthermore, the stage *and* auditorium were lit overall with candles, and the actors had no incentive to withdraw into the lights. Indeed they played before the proscenium upon a projecting stage or apron which was as much as 17 feet deep, making their entrances from four doors actually set into the arch. The downstage entrance of Sheridan's Sir Peter Teazle into the midst of the 'school for scandal' (2. ii) enabled him to throw an aside to the audience immediately:

Ladies, your most obedient. (*Aside*) Mercy on me! here is the whole set! a character dead at every word, I suppose.

The actor got a sight of the spectators almost before he saw the other characters, especially since spectators could sit in the 'pit' or in the galleries and boxes at the sides of the apron and over the doors. Thus although it ceased to be essentially a theatre of three-dimensional playing, it remained an intimate one. It was still a theatre in which

The Restoration theatre

the actors played in the same room as that in which the audience sat.

The importance of scenery is hardly acknowledged by the playwrights of the Restoration, and many sets are used over again merely as a decorative background. But in the eighteenth century the scenes are localized with a little more precision, and there are fewer descriptions of the scene in the dialogue, fewer scene changes, and a less episodic play structure. Over two centuries a different drama emerges, until it falls into the characteristically taut pattern of the modern three-act play.

With the actor playing in the theatre and not in a setting, the drama of Dryden, Congreve, Goldsmith, Sheridan and their contemporaries is a strange mixture of realism and non-realism. The properties are bare aids to acting—a table, a chair, a screen. Occasionally a property may have a deeper significance, and the screen in *The School for Scandal* appropriately suggests all that is hidden behind the façade of Lady Teazle's gay insolence, Joseph's hypocrisy and social pretension in general; but properties are not there in any sense for 'atmosphere', a purely modern concept. More detail of real life was presented, but usually with little attempt at natural dialogue and delivery.

In the comedies of the eighteenth century delicious situations of great comic invention involve the audience in a kind of conspiracy with the author as their complications multiply, and the aside becomes his strongest theatrical trick for drawing the audience into the play—what fun Shaw might have had if such a weapon had been at his command! In Goldsmith's *She Stoops to Conquer* Tony Lumpkin's teasing of Mrs Hardcastle over the theft of her jewels, and Kate's little game of deception with the awkward Marlow; in *The School for Scandal* Sir Oliver's disguise as little Premium to test his nephew Charles, and the rightly famous 'screen scene'; in Sheridan's *The Rivals* the reading of 'Beverley's' letter to Lydia in the presence of her aunt Mrs Malaprop, and the deception by Captain Absolute of his father: these are the key scenes in these comedies, and they are dependent for their rare delight upon the ironic thrust and power of the aside.

There is one element in the theatre of this time which should not be under-estimated: the presence of actresses for the first time on the English stage with the restoration of Charles II. In this intimate theatre both they and their audience were conscious of their sex. Shakespeare's plays were rewritten to stress this new range of interest: in *King Lear* Cordelia gained a love-scene with Edgar, and in *The Tempest* Caliban gained a sister; Miranda was multiplied by two, so that two women having never seen a man 'might the more illustrate and commend each other'. A new comedy, one since delicately labelled 'of manners', specifically explored the theme which is never exhausted: the battle of the sexes. The *dance* of the sexes, however, would better describe its light-footed content.

In modern times

It is not easy to generalize about the modern theatre, the theatre of Henrik Ibsen and Bernard Shaw and their successors, since it includes plays as different as *Murder in the Cathedral* and *A Sleep of Prisoners* written for performance in a church, and *The Playboy of the Western World* and *Juno and the Paycock* written for the tiny stage of the Dublin Abbey Theatre. However, it is true to say that most modern plays are written with the preconception that they will be played within a proscenium arch with its clever scenic and lighting effects, and that any rare exceptions are written with a stimulating, but sometimes perverse, intention of showing what drama can do when it is not coyly withdrawn inside a picture-frame.

No description is needed of what is familiar to most of us, but it is very easy to take for granted a mode of play-writing simply because it happens to be current at the time, and assume that anything else is a primitive fore-runner. Unlike science, art is not progressive. Playgoers of today are conditioned to a particular theatre, as any other playgoers are: but students have the task of seeing the drama of their own day in perspective.

The Victorian and Modern theatre

Since playwrights must write according to the physical limitations of an existing theatre, few today presuppose any direct contact with the spectator. A theatre of scenic illusion instead encourages a naturalistic treatment of subjects. The *characteristic* play of modern times, therefore, is that of the 'box' setting: the drawing-room, the kitchen, the garden or the yard. Dialogue approximates in varying degrees to a normal idiom of speech, and the behaviour of a character is accordingly detailed like a person's in real life.

The 'fourth wall' of the box is supposedly felt to be behind the audience, but this does not necessarily help the spectator to feel at one with the characters. The actor's speech, gesture, movement and grouping depend more and more on his feeling for his part, and less and less on his feeling for the spectator. Playing for the other actors and for himself in this way, the modern actor tends to have a more introspective approach to his work. His withdrawal into an illusory scene leaves the spectator in a characteristically detached position: at the worst he becomes a peeping Tom, sitting in darkness, eavesdropping on the lives of other people, watching 'how the other half lives'. And just as we gossip only about those who are slightly disreputable, so the content of modern plays at times acquires this taint. In aiming to reproduce the sensation of life in some degree, modern drama always runs the risk of being 'small', even trivial.

However, at its best it can compensate for its losses by a sharp technique of a different kind. It can involve us in its action by contrasts of idea and character which, as contrasts, engage our thoughtful attention. In a play like Shaw's *Major Barbara*, Barbara's great choice between an idealistic and a practical religion is brilliantly and forcefully *dramatized* in the lively scene in the Salvation Army shelter, and then the rest of the play is spent in engaging us in the dialectics which lead to her decision. In T. S. Eliot's *The Cocktail Party*, sinners grow into saints of one kind or another, while the argument of the play compels us to feel and to reason how and why this has happened.

We are drawn into a 'discussion' with the author who is concerned to place evidence on the stage before us.

It is not difficult to understand the developments that the new actor-audience relationship encouraged. In the remarkable movement towards naturalism, the greatest risk of failure for writers of melodrama lay in not seeming true to life, whereas, before, this was never in question. Thus, in presenting his subjects, Galsworthy must be at great pains to establish his characters as living people and fill in the social background of their lives, in order to win our co-operation in the adventure of performance. Think of his careful portraits of each individual and his mood among the directors of the Trenartha Tin Plate Works in *Strife*, or the contrasted detail of the living conditions of the Barthwicks and the Joneses in *The Silver Box*, or the closely observed decorum of the solicitor's office in *Justice*. Naturalism may involve the dramatist in awkward compromises with people and situations, since drama must always make order out of life, and the stage can never be wholly real. But if we do 'participate' in a modern play, we do it in a new way.

The Shakespearian sequence of scenes, which followed an impressionistic and emotional pattern, now gives place to a tighter, logical structure. Interest is sustained by a steady pressure of events to the end, broken only by the falling of the curtain on thrilling action at the end of each act, designed to keep the spectator in his seat and not let him slip away home (the so-called 'strong curtain'). The argument of the play may remain unresolved till the last possible moment, like the detective story which keeps us guessing until the last page; in an Elizabethan play like *Hamlet* we have always known or anticipated the outcome. In some of the better naturalistic plays, we may never be told who is on the side of the angels, just as we are never quite sure whether Barbara or Undershaft her father is in the right. In the very best modern tragicomedies, like Shaw's *Saint Joan* and O'Casey's *The Plough and the Stars*, the audience can be spiritually involved: not just the jury, but the prisoner in the dock.

Greek

Medieval

Elizabethan

Restoration

Modern

Diagram to illustrate the change in the actor and audience relationship

The split between the worlds of actor and audience affects the conduct of comedy. In Goldsmith's *She Stoops to Conquer*, we share Tony Lumpkin's pleasure in deceiving Marlow and Hastings by sending them to an imaginary 'Buck's Head' which is in fact his own house; in the famous tea-party of Shaw's *Pygmalion*, we laugh but remain aloof. Indeed, there is as much pleasure in mocking Eliza Doolittle with her 'small talk' about an aunt 'done in' for the sake of a missing straw hat, as there is in mocking the Eynsford Hills who swallow the story hook, line and sinker. At the height of laughter or of tension, the modern dramatist risks a divided audience, and a divided audience implies a spectator divided in his mind. Such a spectator is one who may not be completely controlled by the play.

When we take up the text of a play, we therefore ask this question: what kind of theatrical vitality would this play have had in its own time? To understand a play is to *undergo* it.

3   Words and voices

Feeling and meaning

The playwright knows that in the theatre he has our
ears, and much of his appeal rests upon the feeling he
wants us to hear in the *voices* of his actors, as distinct from
the meaning of their words. He knows that in the human
voice he has a most musical and flexible instrument.
Bernard Shaw used to mark his production script with
musical terms as a personal reminder of the contrast and
variety he wanted from his performers. William Poel, who
tried to re-create an Elizabethan style of performance for
Shakespeare, spent several weeks rehearsing his players
in what he called their 'tunes', expecting an actor to be
able to cover two octaves in the speaking of a sentence, and
casting the parts as opera is cast: thus for *Twelfth Night*,
Viola was a mezzo-soprano, Olivia a contralto, Maria a
high soprano; Orsino was tenor to Malvolio's baritone, and
Sir Toby was bass to Sir Andrew Aguecheek's falsetto.

We may find this approach amusing, but at least it
acknowledges that a good writer carefully creates the
speech of his characters, and indeed whole scenes, with
a musical ear, since the musical variety of dramatic
dialogue is an essential part of its interest. Reading a play
silently encourages us to ignore this and to hear it tone-
lessly.

Try a simple experiment. Imagine you hear a footstep,
and then say the words 'I hear him coming' in as many
different ways as possible. You will not be able to exhaust
the number of suggestions thrown out by your changes of
vocal inflexion, suggestions about your character, the
character of your visitor and the situation between the two
of you. What elements in the voice achieve this variety?

They reduce to five, which one must train oneself to recognize in the words on the page, just as a musician reads a score. Remember them as:

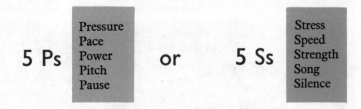

| **5 Ps** | Pressure
Pace
Power
Pitch
Pause | **or** | **5 Ss** | Stress
Speed
Strength
Song
Silence |

As an expression of joy by someone who has been waiting a long time, 'I hear him coming' might *stress* the last word, be spoken in the rapid and increasing *pace* of excitement, be reduced in *strength* to a whisper proportionate to the excitement, and rise to a higher *pitch* according to the quality of the happiness anticipated. A degree of 'non-speech' may accompany the words, perhaps a *pause* of intense realization preceding them. How would these five ingredients vary if the situation demanded an expression of fear, or grief, or indifference?

If the mere noise of speech can permit such variety in meaning, a dramatist has the task of bringing his dialogue under control, making it mean what he alone wishes. We can indeed measure the quality of a writer's words by the extent to which he arranges their sound. A prose dramatist ensures that character and situation are so precisely established that even a colloquial phrase has particularity. A verse dramatist has the easier task, in that he can accurately reproduce in the movement of the verse the shifting of a mind, the exhibition of an emotion, or even of an action, as when we speak aloud the line in which Shakespeare's Richard II breaks his mirror,

For there it is, *crack'd* in an hundred shivers (4. i),

we know exactly when the mirror is smashed.

The following simple system of signs can be used to mark a text, and will help one to read with the voice of one's ideal imagining:

A simple notation for dramatic expression

pressure	underlining, or double underlining for greater emphasis	<u>rank</u> and <u><u>gross</u></u>	stress
pace	acceleration: an arrow above the words deceleration: an arrow reversed the pace of a whole speech or sequence of speeches by arrows in the margin	⟶ oh fie, fie ⟵ O God, O God	speed
power	the musical signs for crescendo and diminuendo in volume of sound	cres. the Everlasting dim. grows to seed	strength
pitch	pointers above the word(s) on which the inflexion falls	in nature (rising) possess it merely (falling)	song
pause	a stroke across the line, doubled for a longer silence	not so much; | not two ||	silence

As an example of the control that can be exercised by a verse dramatist, the following is a likely reading of part of Hamlet's first soliloquy, suggesting his anguish and weariness at the beginning of the play:

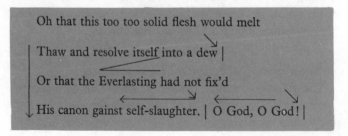

Oh that this too too solid flesh would melt

Thaw and resolve itself into a dew \|

Or that the Everlasting had not fix'd

His canon gainst self-slaughter. \| O God, O God! \|

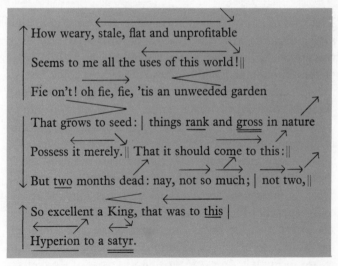

Verse controlling voice in *Hamlet*

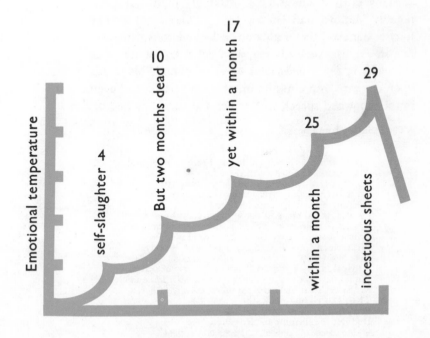

The pattern of a soliloquy from *Hamlet*

The kind of stress on words like *unweeded*, *rank*, *gross* and *satyr*, coupled with the images of disgust, decay and corruption, will suggest Hamlet's bitter tone as he thinks of the situation at Elsinore. Starting almost colourlessly, the speech quickly acquires shape and tempo by moving through consecutive 'fever points' (of which two minor ones already appear in the lines quoted), and the pattern of the whole speech* can be represented by a graph (p. 41).

We notice incidentally that Shakespeare seems to mark these points of crisis by his repetition of *two months*, *within a month*, *within a month*, and this kind of study of his speeches reveals that he composed each one with a musical shape of its own. But Shakespeare is not alone in his awareness of the contribution the actor's voice can make: in English dramatic writing the plays of Congreve, Shaw and O'Casey, pre-eminently, will bear such analysis with interesting results.

Many great dramatists fail strikingly in this respect, notably Marlowe and Galsworthy. It may seem strange to cite Marlowe, the originator of the sonorous, 'mighty' line in English verse drama, as a colourless writer, but especially in the *Tamburlaine* plays he pounds his words upon our ears with a minimum of vocal variety, and even in the renowned speech with which Faustus is carried off

* The soliloquy continues:

>   so loving to my mother,
> That he might not beteem the winds of heaven
> Visit her face too roughly. Heaven and earth
> Must I remember: why she would hang on him,
> As if increase of appetite had grown
> By what it fed on; and yet within a month!
> Let me not think on't: Frailty, thy name is woman.
> A little month, or ere those shoes were old,
> With which she followed my poor father's body
> Like Niobe, all tears. Why she, even she,
> (O Heaven! A beast that wants discourse of reason
> Would have mourn'd longer) married with mine uncle,
> My father's brother: But no more like my father,
> Than I to Hercules. Within a month!
> Ere yet the salt of most unrighteous tears
> Had left the flushing of her galled eyes,
> She married. O most wicked speed, to post
> With such dexterity to incestuous sheets:
> It is not, nor it cannot come to good.
> But break my heart, for I must hold my tongue.

to Hell, his shrill tone lacks dramatic contrast. Galsworthy hardly bears out the idea that, in being heightened, all dramatic speech must have the touch of the poet: the dullness of Galsworthy's ear is one of the reasons why his plays have had so short a life.

However, it is generally true that the convention of poetic drama permits far more emotion on the surface, and therefore more vocal music, than in naturalistic drama. Lear curses his daughter Goneril with the intensity of sound and imagery of

> infect her beauty,
> You fen-suck'd fogs, drawn by the powerful sun,
> To fall, and blister.

In Galsworthy's *Strife* much of the feeling remains hidden: when Edgar Anthony suggests mercy to the strikers, his father turns on him with a more subdued, but equally vehement turn of phrase for the manner of the play:

These are the words of my own son. They are the words of a generation I don't understand; the words of a soft breed.

Kind of play	Example	Speech	Feeling tends to be	Pace tends to be
poetic drama	Shakespeare Jonson	lyrical, rhetorical	on the surface	faster
comedy of manners	Congreve Sheridan	mannered, stylized	sharply contrasted in dialogue and aside	variable
naturalistic drama	Ibsen Galsworthy	colloquial	beneath the surface	slower

A rough guide to the effect of convention on the quality of the dialogue

Hearing tones and contrasts

Even when we have learned to hear the tune of a speech, there is more to listen for. Drama does not exist alone in the single voice, but in the interplay of character with character; 'rhythm is meaning' is a rule that applies especially to the building of speech upon speech. This in turn raises questions of the growth of contrast between characters, their relationship with each other at any particular moment in the play, and the direction and speed in which a scene is progressing. These questions are answered in the theatre by contrasts in vocal *tones*, by the *timing* of consecutive speeches (or the precise speed with which one speech follows another), and by the general *tempo* (or the varying rate at which speeches or actions reach the spectator). These are more than technical matters: the good dramatist in his words accurately anticipates what his actors must do. So, too, the student will be aware of a musical pattern in the dialogue if a scene is to live.

In every duologue the contrast of tones is certain to be different. The range from a complete harmony between two characters to a sharp opposition of feeling is infinite. Moreover, each contrast is individual because of differences of character and sex, the situation as presented and its point of development.

The well-known interrogation of Jack Worthing by Lady Bracknell in *The Importance of Being Earnest* shows an extreme contrast well suited to the quality of farcical comedy found in this play. Lady Bracknell has been conceived by Wilde as a gross type of social snob, and to accentuate her snobbery, he arranges that the young man who is to ask her daughter's hand in marriage shall be, as we remember, not only without the 'right' parents, but without parents at all. She is scandalized in the following way:

JACK. . . . The fact is, Lady Bracknell, I said I had lost my
    parents. It would be nearer the truth to say that my
    parents seem to have lost me. . . . I don't actually know
    who I am by birth. I was . . . well, I was found.
LADY BRACKNELL. Found!

JACK. The late Mr Thomas Cardew, an old gentleman of a very charitable and kindly disposition, found me, and gave me the name of Worthing, because he happened to have a first-class ticket for Worthing in his pocket at the time. Worthing is a place in Sussex. It is a seaside resort.

LADY BRACKNELL. Where did the charitable gentleman who had a first-class ticket for this seaside resort find you?

JACK (*gravely*). In a hand-bag.

LADY BRACKNELL. A hand-bag?

JACK (*very seriously*). Yes, Lady Bracknell. I was in a hand-bag—a somewhat large, black leather hand-bag, with handles to it—an ordinary hand-bag in fact.

LADY BRACKNELL. In what locality did this Mr James, or Thomas, Cardew come across this ordinary hand-bag?

JACK. In the cloak-room at Victoria Station. It was given to him in mistake for his own.

LADY BRACKNELL. The cloak-room at Victoria Station?

JACK. Yes. The Brighton line.

LADY BRACKNELL. The line is immaterial.

45

If we listen in imagination to the sounds of these two voices, we hear two contrapuntal movements of speech. Jack, standing beside the stiff-backed lady with his knees knocking, is speaking with more and more hesitation, taking his cues more and more slowly as he fears for everything he says; his statements become more confused to the point of the ridiculous. As for Lady Bracknell, the horror in her voice is unmistakable with each new revelation, and through *found . . . a hand-bag . . . the cloak-room at Victoria Station* to *the line is immaterial*, pitch and pressure will indicate her rising indignation. Unlike Jack's, her feelings come nearer and nearer the surface as she explodes upon her cues and reduces Jack to jelly.

This duologue, then, has finely represented a relationship between two characters in vocal as well as verbal terms. Other varieties of vocal vitality are worth examining in the duologues between, for example:

Rosalind and Orlando: *As You Like It*, 3. ii and 4. i.
Viola and Orsino: *Twelfth Night*, 2. iv.
Brutus and Cassius: *Julius Caesar*, 4. iii.
Hamlet and Gertrude: *Hamlet*, 3. iv.
Othello and Iago: *Othello*, 3. iii and 4. i.
Volpone and Mosca: *Volpone; or, The Fox*, act 1.
Sir Peter and Lady Teazle: *The School for Scandal*, 2. i and 3. i.
Dick Dudgeon and Judith: *The Devil's Disciple*, act 2.
Bluntschli and Raina: *Arms and the Man*, act 1.
Christy and Pegeen: *The Playboy of the Western World*, act 1.

These are exchanges that linger in the memory.

Pace and tempo

The example from *The Importance of Being Earnest* suggests that, along with the need to hear vocal tones and contrasts, the effort must be made to judge the particular tempo in which a scene is written. Again, every case is unique.

Verse provides a strong guide in this respect, since the verse dramatist is free to use a striking vocal music to stress his intentions. In the beautifully varied duet between Macbeth and Lady Macbeth after the murder of King Duncan, Shakespeare whips up the terror and the pace by this curt dialogue:

MACBETH. Didst thou not hear a noise?
LADY MACBETH. I heard the owl scream, and the crickets cry. Did not you speak?
MACBETH. When?
LADY MACBETH. Now.
MACBETH. As I descended?
LADY MACBETH. Ay.

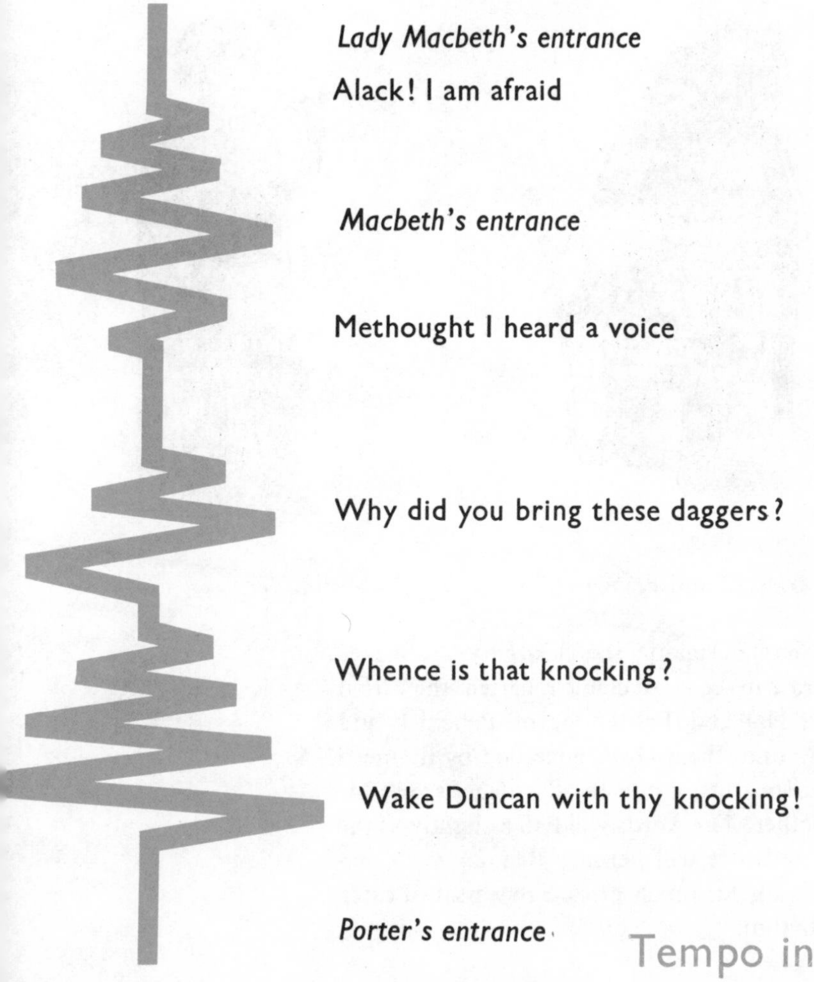

Lady Macbeth's entrance

Alack! I am afraid

Macbeth's entrance

Methought I heard a voice

Why did you bring these daggers?

Whence is that knocking?

Wake Duncan with thy knocking!

Porter's entrance

Tempo in *Macbeth*

But as fear penetrates Macbeth's mind, as his conscience obsesses him, Shakespeare restrains our racing minds with the slow, throbbing tones of

> Methought I heard a voice cry, 'Sleep no more:
> Macbeth does murther sleep', the innocent sleep,
> Sleep that knits up the ravell'd sleave of care . . .

This violent variation in tempo expresses the action on the stage, reveals the feelings of the characters and controls the response of the spectator.

Falstaff and Prince Hal

Nor is there any mistaking the flexibility of Shakespeare's rapid prose in scenes of comic repartee: the verbal duels of Prince Hal and Falstaff or of Benedick and Beatrice are laws unto themselves, governed by the need to point a witticism, turn a pun to advantage, score one character off another. The words will trip as lightly as the laughter of the audience will permit. Reading such dialogue to oneself calls for much private rehearsal to catch its swing and rhythm.

A sense of the dance of the words is especially needed for the comedy of the Restoration and of Goldsmith and Sheridan. In this the sparkle and elegance of the phraseology demand that the sounds flow with as great a range of vocal colour as rapid delivery will allow, and that thoughts be suddenly illuminated by precipitate flashes of pace. The scandal scene of Sheridan's play scintillates with the thrust and parry felt in a multiple series of little pressures, each marked by a quick rejoinder of laughter, until general laughter tops a climax of quips. When Mrs Candour proposes poor Miss Vermilion for ridicule by saying, 'She has a charming fresh colour', the ball is passed from one character to the next after this fashion:

Speaker	Preparation (ebb)	The Quip (flow)	Laughter response
Lady Teazle	Yes,	when it is fresh put on.	!
Mrs Candour	Oh, fie! I'll swear her colour is natural:	I have seen it come and go!	!!
Lady Teazle	I dare swear you have, ma'am:	it goes off at night, and comes again in the morning.	!!!
Sir Benjamin Backbite	True, ma'am, it not only comes and goes;	but, what's more, egad, her maid can fetch and carry it!	!!!!

Analysis of Sheridan's dialogue

And so the scandal-mongers strip Mrs Evergreen, the Widow Ochre, Miss Simper and the rest. This 'ebb and flow' can be seen in a gesture of the arm or fan, and the inclination of the body as well: elegance of bearing exactly matches elegance of language.

The School for Scandal

After Shakespeare and Sheridan, the plays of Bernard Shaw offer a mine of successful experiments in controlled tempo; but these the reader will wish to discover for himself.

Verse or prose?

Arguments about the playwright's use of verse in preference to prose, or vice versa, slip more easily into place in the light of what has been said in this chapter.

It is true that in Elizabethan drama central and well-born characters often speak in verse, where minor or low-born characters speak in prose. Yet this is a rule broken so often as to be no rule at all: Falstaff is a pivotal character and a knight, but speaks no verse; Prince Hal will not speak verse when he is with Falstaff. This suggests that verse is used, not so much to identify character, but to mark the *convention of feeling* required by each scene.

We can say that prose brings us down to earth: Hal shows us the natural man in the Boar's Head tavern, and when we are there, he and Falstaff are dramatically set against the formal politicians. It is thus of greater importance to recognize that, within the framework of Elizabethan poetic drama, the spectator will accept a large variety of style and mood. The playwright uses this to stimulate the audience to make imaginative leaps as the theme demands.

A playwright does not write in verse merely to decorate a prosaic subject. He does so partly because the audience expects or permits it, and chiefly because he wishes to take advantage of the extended range of speech that verse affords. But dramatic verse must stand the test of being an efficient vehicle for the voice, gesture and movement of the actor: it must be capable of being *particular* and *resourceful* for stage action. If the verse idiom can be all these, then it offers the play and its actors a greater scope for truly theatrical expression.

A century after Shakespeare, Addison chose to write his *Cato* in verse because a noble theme demanded noble language. Furthermore, he anticipated the services of an actor declaiming in the solemn tones which Thomas Betterton had made the vogue. But majesty of speech is not enough to create dramatic life, as a glance at Cato's long soliloquy on death will show. Cato is described as 'sitting in a thoughtful posture. In his hand is Plato's book on the Immortality of the Soul. A drawn sword on the table by him.'

> It must be so—Plato, thou reason'st well!—
> Else whence this pleasing hope, this fond desire,
> This longing after immortality?
> Or whence this secret dread, and inward horror,
> Of falling into nought? . . .

In spite of the tempestuous idea, the sonorous regularity of these lines admits none of the hesitations and twists of a human mind. By its virtually unvarying rhythm, tone and pace, Addison's verse deprives his character of vitality.

51

Contrast the Hamlet who speaks a soliloquy on a similar theme:

> To be or not to be, that is the question.

Shakespeare did *not* write a regular

> To be or not to be, is that the question?

so that even in this first famous line, with its two heavy stresses *bé thát* unexpectedly thrust together, we hear the catching of Hamlet's breath and some of the quality of his feeling.

For the Women of Canterbury in *Murder in the Cathedral*, T. S. Eliot created a *choric* language based often upon twentieth century rhythms of speech. It was a language which was at the same time a sensuous poetry wooing his audience towards the feeling the play wanted, carrying a useful range of vocal tones, and providing a full set of signals for group movement. Notice how the macabre chorus of terror which precedes the murder of Thomas à Becket, 'I have smelt them, the death bringers', invites a division of its lines into 'light' (high) and 'dark' (low) voices. Notice how the scream that follows the killing is expressed in the first line by high-pitched phrases which expect separate cries and individual running movements:

> Clear the air! clean the sky! wash the wind! take stone from stone and wash them.

In the second line darker voices are heard from another direction, voices which perhaps suggest that bodies are huddling in fear:

> The land is foul, the water is foul, our beasts and ourselves defiled with blood.

How to play the right variations with differently toned voices in different combinations is one of the challenges of producing Eliot's remarkable chorus.

So a dramatist chooses a particular verse form because it can be flexible, accommodating both a rhetorical and a colloquial idiom. This partly accounts for the kind of verse Eliot tried to develop for his later plays, and for the great success of the blank iambic verse of the Elizabethan theatre.

But the proviso should be added that prose need not prevent the dramatist from creating 'poetic' impressions of life. In modern times the great European prose dramatists, Ibsen and Chekhov, Strindberg and Pirandello, O'Casey and Brecht, have all broken through the barriers of realism which a belittling prose dialogue seems to set up. It is not the words alone which make the play, but the vivid dramatic impressions which the words can create.

4   How real is a character?

Convention and the actor

The title of this chapter is not as foolish as it may seem. It is easy for the spectator to be misled in his understanding of a character's function when that character is endowed with the living personality of an actor, and even the reader hearing his own or some other familiar voice reading aloud has the sensation of an actual person embodying the part. But it is unwise to ignore the fact that *no* character can ever be wholly real, as real as oneself with an infinite complexity of big and little thoughts and feelings, motives and purposes, good points and bad. Some playwrights may, indeed, try deliberately to make their people *seem* as lifelike as this while the play is in progress; but others will have no such intention.

It is, however, natural to wish to take a character out of his context in a play or a scene, and then to think and talk about him as if he had an existence apart: yet this practice will always lead us to find the author in some respect falling short of being lifelike in his character-drawing. Again, it is easy to be misled, because a playwright must, of course, call upon some aspects of human life: his actor must be able to move and speak in a recognizably human way, and the character must be an efficient agent for the purposes of the play. For drama is essentially about human beings: even the unnaturally villainous Iago must use the ways of a human being to tempt his victim Othello.

Therefore it is important to weigh up in each case how little or how much truth to life we may reasonably ask of a character. One must put the simple question: if I were playing this part, how much reality would be expected of me to make the play work? The answer to this, every time, depends upon *the convention of the play*, the tacit agreement with the audience about how much make-believe is allowable. Convention has changed constantly through the history of drama, and we who read a play today must be ready to modify our demands on a character who was created at some point in the past.

Character in Greek and medieval times

The central characters of ancient Greek tragedy were generally those of kings and heroes, superhuman figures prepared to face enormous odds, idealized beings who might for the space of the play stand for all mankind. They challenged the gods in order to demonstrate the littleness and the greatness of man. In such circumstances the details of individual psychology (whether Agamemnon truly loved his wife Clytemnestra before she murdered him, or whether Oedipus might have a sense of humour about the series of coincidences that led to his downfall) were not only uncalled for, but would positively have stood in the way of the stark presentation of the issues and the universal impact of the tragedy.

We have seen how the size of the Greek theatre demanded rhetorical speech and grand, unreal acting. Individuality in the acting was further suppressed by the grotesque, ritualistic mask, which conveyed only the fixed facial expression of eyes and mouth whereby the hero's state could be identified at great distance. In tragedy, such a mask lent immense dignity to the actor, but wholly denied him the chance to develop as a real person. This is not a weakness in the drama; rather, a degree of unreality was essential for an impersonal reverence to be accorded to the play's subject.

A character in a medieval morality play was not obliged to create the heroic vision of the Greek religious and community drama, but for other reasons his role was also fixed from the start, offering no chance of character development. The morality figure, a physical or moral attribute like Beauty or Understanding, was a constant, like the symbol 'x' used in making an equation in algebra. Every character in the morality was expected to make a sharp moral point, so that there was no doubt about the good or bad in him, and no distraction from the quality he stood for. The lesson to be taught, for example, by one of the Seven Deadly Sins (Pride, Envy, Sloth, Greed, Avarice, Anger and Lust) had to be simple and clear-cut. But such a character stood only for some part of a set of moral rules acceptable in the Middle Ages, and we must be acquainted with these. In almost every respect his character was scarcely like that of a real person, nor should we expect it to be. Just as in this kind of abstract play naturalistic behaviour was largely out of place, so too was naturalistic characterization. A morality figure must first be *functional*.

Thus truth to human psychology was at a minimum, although this does not necessarily mean that a morality character was a bore. When Everyman, from the fifteenth-century play of that name, is warned to prepare for his last journey by the gruesome figure of Death, Fellowship at first displays a jolly geniality and agrees to join him. When Everyman explains that from this journey there is no returning, Fellowship, amusingly, finds excuses and will have nothing to do with the proposal. Cousin, in her turn, complains of cramp in the toe, and declares herself unable to travel. Thus there is some survival of the quality that made the mystery plays such lively drama. Subtlety is largely missing from virtuous figures like Good Deeds, who consents to go with Everyman when she is freed by the confession of his sins. Even Everyman himself, who must symbolize the simplicity of faith, tends to lack human warmth. Yet it is the very simplicity and clarity of this drama that is the source of its vigour and pathos, and its strength as an exciting theatre experience.

In Shakespeare

Some of this straightforward morality symbolism survives in the drama of the Elizabethans, and in part explains the function of their characterization. Hotspur at times assumes the role of Pride, Angelo of Hypocrisy, Iago of the 'Vice', the stock medieval figure of devilish fun; Macbeth can be seen as Ambition, Leontes Jealousy, and so on. Even Faustus, Lear and Hamlet take on some of the universal qualities we associate with 'Everyman' or 'Mankynd'. Whole scenes may be built up according to the morality pattern of the contest between the good and evil facets of man's mind: in the first scene of *Doctor Faustus*, Marlowe unashamedly introduces a Good Angel and an Evil Angel to speak for Faustus's conscience. The debate of the Greeks in *Troilus and Cressida* is simplified if we recognize Achilles as Pride and 'blockish Ajax' as Vanity; and contradictions in the character of Cressida are to some extent explained by her role as Faithlessness.

This link with the past is mentioned first, since a central character in an Elizabethan poetic drama frequently displays a *representative* quality, whereby he seems to stand for common human feelings in mankind as a whole. This it is never wise to ignore. But such an approach will not explain Shakespeare for long, since he uses a stock figure as at most a peg upon which to hang a more intricate web of human motivation.

It is important also to understand that, although Elizabethan convention demanded that a character be *consistent*, he need not always be *convincing*. A character in an Elizabethan tragedy had both to play the scene and to engineer the mechanics of the performance. This sometimes produced unreal results, as when Horatio must conjure up the dawn over Hamlet's Elsinore, or Queen Gertrude give a graphic eyewitness description of Ophelia's drowning. At other times, Shakespeare will turn this convention to great ironic advantage, as when the unsuspecting Duncan finds that Macbeth's castle 'hath a pleasant seat', or when the veteran Enobarbus grows lyrical about Cleopatra. The outstanding example of 'unreality' was the soliloquy; but, though incredible in itself, it allowed the dramatist to force upon his plot a sudden leap forward, or to grant his character an urgent revelation of depth.

In Elizabethan tragedy, however, conventions of characterization are fairly straightforward: a hero is heroic, a villain is villainous, and might be expected to remain so —though exceptions can be found, as when the Duchess of Malfi and her executioner Bosola both suffer a change of heart, and Lear and Macbeth amazingly anticipate more modern experiments in showing the manner in which men may grow. In the comedy, irregularities in behaviour on the stage are more disconcerting. We may inquire why Rosalind does not go straight to her father in the Forest of Arden; or why Viola, upon hearing that Orsino is unmarried, decides to join his service while still gasping from the shipwreck; or why Bassanio fails to recognize the disguised Portia when face to face with her in court. The answer each time must be, to satisfy the requirements of the plot. Yet there is no desire to ask such questions once Shakespeare's comedy has begun to create the fantasy which can admit heroines who change their sex or heroes who fall in love at first sight. He fashions a world of pantomime in order that the pretty absurdities of human behaviour may be gently mocked.

If we allow Shakespeare his unreal tragic and comic frameworks, and his larger-than-life portraits of men and women, we grant him the licence to create subtleties of character which have yet to be matched. The Shakespearian character is no puppet. For Rosalind and Viola may act strangely by natural standards, as does the Lear who casts out a beloved daughter after many years' intimate acquaintance with her true qualities; but in other respects they disclose a complexity of mind and a vitality of spirit which suggests their author's penetrating understanding of people. In *Much Ado About Nothing*, for example, Benedick and Beatrice may seem at first glance to be figures from a comedy of manners, but come to play them, and it is quickly appreciated that a deep sense of their psychology is wanted if the great humour of their situation is to emerge. This quality in Shakespeare has astonished psychologists in modern times, and will fascinate his readers always.

58

So it is reasonable to look to the convention of the play to explain the kind of character when it is Greek tragedy or medieval morality drama, but in Shakespeare the blending and overlapping of different forms of characterization make this a limiting approach. Dr Johnson declared that Shakespeare 'caught his ideas from the living world', and it is his genius for offering more than the conventions demand which sets him apart from his contemporaries and successors. It is unlikely to be right, but it *is* possible to play Othello or Shylock or Brutus as if they belonged to a modern 'kitchen sink' play: to be able even to attempt the Russian-American 'Method' kind of acting for Shakespeare, by which an actor must immerse himself in his part, is to acknowledge that Shakespeare's characters possess life in abundance.

In Ben Jonson

The comic characters of Ben Jonson do not have Shakespeare's touch of sympathetic understanding, and this was partly because Jonson cultivated a restricting theory of comedy and character-drawing. Against every English precedent, he tried to fit to the English stage the classical theory of comedy which served dramatists like the Greek Menander and the Romans Plautus and Terence. This advocated that drama should 'instruct by pleasing', and in particular that comedy should 'strip the ragged follies of the time/Naked as at their birth' (from the Induction to *Everyman Out of his Humour*). The exaggeration and satirizing of character was his chief weapon, and to make his intentions plain to his contemporaries he borrowed the naïve medieval medical concept of the four 'humours' or fluids in the body (the sanguine, choleric, phlegmatic and melancholy) that mix to determine a person's dominating trait. He then worked this together with character types like the jealous husband or the boastful soldier borrowed from the Roman comedy, and with some of the racily personified sins and vices of the native morality drama.

Essentially, his approach was that of the caricaturist, or,

in modern journalism, the cartoonist, who exaggerates dominant features for quick recognition and sharp ridicule.

The ordinary figures created by the caricaturist, like Jonson's, have been labelled 'types', and a *typed* character is one who stands often for only a single aspect of man's nature.

He also borrowed the convenient morality tradition of identifying a character by the name of his quality, as Shakespeare did for the clowns in *A Midsummer Night's Dream* and *Henry IV, Part II*. Thus, from *Everyman In his Humour*, Old Knowell is the father who knows too much about his son's activities, and George Downright is 'a plain squire' who speaks his mind too frankly. Brainworm (like Jonson's other 'parasites', Mosca the Fly in *Volpone* and double-faced Face in *The Alchemist*) is the sly, scheming serving-man who contrives the intrigues of the plot, with the serpent ('worm') of the Devil in his brain. Perhaps the English parasite derives more from the medieval Vice than from the rascally Roman servant. This same tradition serves the Restoration comedians with fops like Etherege's Sir Fopling Flutter and Vanbrugh's Lord Foppington, and with indecorous elderly ladies like Lady Wishfor't; and in the eighteenth century it serves Sheridan with Mrs Malaprop, Lady Teazle and the rest. Even Shaw is not past colouring our impression of his characters with names, for example, like Captain Bluntschli, Andrew Undershaft and Alfred Doolittle.

Yet we should not trouble ourselves too much about the theory of humours: in devising grotesque situations to accentuate the absurdities of his characters, Jonson's intuitive wit and sense of theatre quickly abandoned theory. In Captain Bobadill in *Everyman In his Humour* and Volpone the Fox, who dupes the harpies who come begging to his pretended sick-bed, we find characters who are far from being rigid cardboard creatures. Bobadill is the boasting coward, but, sharing some of Falstaff's nerve, he never loses his dignity when his tall stories are exposed. Even when Downright cudgels him upon his refusal to

Captain Bobadill

fight, the gallant captain bounces up at the first opportunity with a plausible line of defence:

Well, gentlemen, bear witness, I was bound to the peace, by this good day;

and again,

I never sustained the like disgrace, by Heaven! sure I was struck with a planet thence, for I had no power to touch my weapon.

This is true comedy. Nevertheless, in spite of this vivid dramatic life, we may not expect these characters to share the many-sided and subtly shaded complexity of real people; nor would such treatment sharpen the satire, any more than the pathetic qualities in Malvolio and Shylock helped to clarify Shakespeare's intentions. Jonson's characters rightly remain predictable and essentially simple, and their humours are all they need to justify their behaviour: once a Bobadill always a Bobadill.

In the comedy of manners

Although humours largely disappeared from the stage with Jonson, the Restoration comedy of manners involved only a slight modification in the method of character creation. In the caricaturing of the upper-class figures which recur throughout this comedy, Jonson's satirical gusto is more delicately controlled and his social range vastly reduced, while Molière's keen observation of human behaviour is borrowed from France for English society.

Each character in the comedy demonstrated a form of behaviour that was there for the audience's inspection and critical judgment:

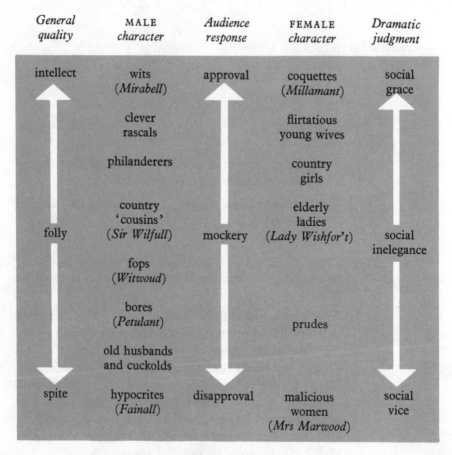

General quality	MALE character	Audience response	FEMALE character	Dramatic judgment
intellect	wits (*Mirabell*)	approval	coquettes (*Millamant*)	social grace
	clever rascals		flirtatious young wives	
	philanderers		country girls	
folly	country 'cousins' (*Sir Wilfull*)	mockery	elderly ladies (*Lady Wishfor't*)	social inelegance
	fops (*Witwoud*)			
	bores (*Petulant*)		prudes	
	old husbands and cuckolds			
spite	hypocrites (*Fainall*)	disapproval	malicious women (*Mrs Marwood*)	social vice

A sliding scale of Restoration comic values

With examples from characters in Congreve's *The Way of the World*

Characters are arranged in each play almost as if to present a pattern or microcosm of society. They are drawn according to whether they were less or more desirable as companions and lovers, husbands and wives. To suggest this is of course to over-simplify, and not every type of person appears in every play; moreover, it is possible to discover characters who are rather more than types—thus Mirabell, who is in love with Millamant in Congreve's *The Way of the World*, declares that 'for a discerning man' he is 'somewhat too passionate a lover; for I like her with all her faults; nay, like her for her faults'. A man in love in spite of himself immediately becomes more than a caricature.

However, it is generally true that life is presented in these plays as a kind of gay social game, or a quadrille in which the dancers accept and reject their partners according to the rules of the dance. Nearly all characters behave with an equal propriety of style, the gentlemen with immense wit and elegance, the ladies sparkling in every word and gesture; but we are clearly intended to perceive that some are sociable, others spiteful; some honest, others dishonest; some men fashionable, others effeminate; some to be approved, others mocked. Under these circumstances the plot was of little interest to the spectator, and by the standards of the nineteenth century a 'well-made play' was a casual business indeed: it merely linked the figures together in a temporary relationship. Rather than piece out cause and effect in a sequence of events, the audience was enjoyably occupied in recognizing the characteristics of the players. Each comedy became, as it were, a dramatized trial of society's transgressors, judged according to the laws of social decorum obtaining at the time.

It again follows that these characters have little life, apart from the design of artificial manners into which they are fitted: we do not ask whether Millamant can cook. And any comment on Restoration comedy must stress the lightness of touch with which the trial was conducted. There is a sense in which the comedy of manners approves, where Jonson's more biting satire criticizes, the values of society.

One last point before this artificial world is dismissed. If we may not ask whether Millamant can cook, in Sheridan's *The School for Scandal* some seventy years later we are *told* that Lady Teazle's daily occupation as a girl was 'to inspect the dairy, superintend the poultry, make extracts from the family receipt-book, and comb my Aunt Deborah's lapdog'. Moreover, in Goldsmith's *She Stoops to Conquer* we are *shown* Kate Hardcastle playing a very recognizable barmaid, if only to win her man. In other words, the characters of eighteenth-century comedy have rather more common life and particular humanity than their seventeenth-century counterparts. The transition to naturalism is a slow process which can be measured over two centuries.

The naturalistic character

For centuries a character was essentially a 'mask', a *dramatis persona*, a representation of humanity or of some aspect of it, and not truly a human being. The naturalistic dramatists of modern times create in another vein. Although there is much naturalistic behaviour to be found in Shakespeare's characters, and much that is deliberately unnatural in, say, Shaw's, for the first time our *conviction* of real life in the character may be important to the success of a play. How may a playwright set about convincing us that a character is real?

First, by individualizing him, convincing us that he is a unique creature with a particular set of qualities and memories and personal relationships. The playwright will provide him with roots to his life, and reasons for what he does, which may be of interest in themselves. The exposition of this kind of background to a character may take up much of the play, though the dramatist's need to preserve a naturalistic surface may lead him to insinuate the information, as it were, between the lines. This procedure may in turn urge a tighter and a 'closed', rather than an 'open', structure upon the play, especially in intensely naturalistic

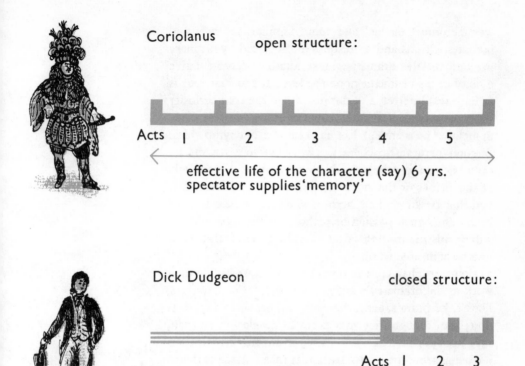

Coriolanus   open structure:

Acts   1   2   3   4   5

effective life of the character (say) 6 yrs.
spectator supplies 'memory'

Dick Dudgeon   closed structure:

Acts   1   2   3

his life 'before the play begins'   24 hrs.
(roots and memories)
actor supplies 'memory'

Diagram to contrast the stage lives of
Shakespeare's Coriolanus and Shaw's
Dick Dudgeon (*The Devil's Disciple*)

drama, in which it would be difficult to make a 'slice of
life' last several years.

Secondly, by carefully avoiding the distortions of high
tragedy and broad comedy; denying, that is, the traditional emphasis of the theatre. The drama must in this

way become 'smaller' and more familiar. Heroes and heroines, clowns and grotesques are replaced by ordinary people: yet the dramatist must retain a representative quality in his character none the less. If the character is to have real interest, and not just invite the cold curiosity which a psychological case-study might, we must be made to feel that he is enough like us to capture our sympathies. A good naturalistic character will therefore not be an eccentric or a psychopath. Nor will he have a monopoly of the virtues or the vices: he will not be wholly good or bad, nor be an obvious hero or villain, but be a little of both. Thus great passion or pathos, revulsion or ridicule, will be missing from this drama, and we shall feel at home in a recognizable world.

However, characters in modern plays must still do their work as the dramatist's agents. Galsworthy's characters, like Shakespeare's, enact the story and provide its motivation; and, though they may seem to develop more than, say, Romeo or Viola, they must remain functional, their job being primarily to give particular meaning to the theme of the play. To an audience intent upon interpreting every detail, any irrelevancies surrounding them will mislead and distract. Thus *consistency* is essential for a naturalistic character too, but of another kind: in the greatest plays of Ibsen and Chekhov, each fine shred of speech or behaviour contributes to the spectator's total impression.

The diagram below lists some of the unspoken questions we put, whether consciously or not, as we scrutinize a naturalistic character in performance. Clearly, we may ask some of these questions at a non-naturalistic play also, but only as the dramatist directs us: since it does not matter how old Hamlet was when an undergraduate at the University of Wittenberg, or how many children Lady Macbeth had, Shakespeare does not press these points. But in the drama that uses the appearances of real life, the dramatist and his actor must be prepared to answer all possible queries, just as when we make an acquaintance in reality, we begin to piece together the jigsaw of details that constitute his life.

Origins	when born: period parents: rich/poor education: success?
Social background	religion and politics nature of work income and social class
Tempera-ment	virtues and vices habits and interests loves and hates
Relations with	wife/husband children and parents friends and relatives, etc.

Some of the questions we ask

How some of the answers are given

Physical	dress: rich/poor make-up: age voice and accent
Exposition by self	direct statement action and reaction what is *not* said and done
Exposition by others	direct statement action and reaction what is *not* said and done
Contrasted with others in	appearance speech action and reaction, etc.

Exposition of a many-sided, naturalistic character

Kinds of character, flat and round

After only a few speeches, a reader or spectator may soon become adept at identifying the kind of character he has to reckon with, and it is convenient to divide characters into the 'flat' and the 'round', or the two- and the three-dimensional, as they are sometimes called. They are flat when they are recognizable and predictable and show us only one aspect of human nature; they are round when they are individual and unpredictable and to be judged as complete beings. From what has been said, it is clearly no disgrace to draw a flat character, as long as he serves his purpose.

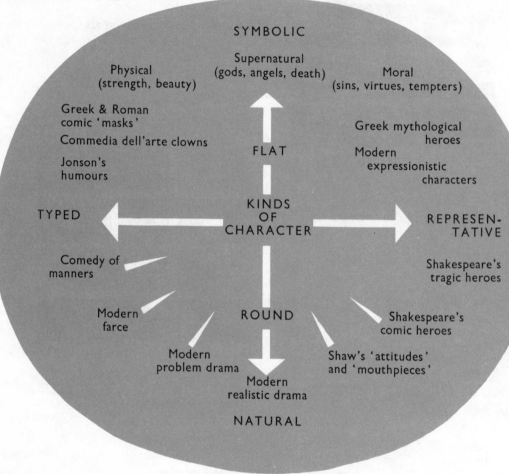

A rough guide to character

However, characters in the greatest drama refuse to be pigeon-holed too easily. We have seen how an abstract morality figure like Fellowship in *Everyman* comes alive with his very natural response to death, how a humour like Jonson's Bobadill or a caricature like Congreve's Mirabell can share the strength of ordinary humanity, or how Shakespeare can give a character an individual psychology. It is especially those categories of stage figures which are representative or typed, and yet which are paradoxically natural and individual, that create the exciting variety of drama. A character like Shylock is the type of the comic avaricious Jew as well as a particular individual capable of calling up sympathy. Lear is a towering giant taking upon himself the sins of the world, and yet at the last he displays a particular father's joy and grief. Even old clowns like Shallow and Silence in minor parts from *Henry IV, Part II* may take on touching human qualities. Shaw's Joan has the personality of a vivacious tomboy while she is also the author's spokesman for protestantism and nationalism.

On the other hand, in many a modern naturalistic play a flat character may destroy the play's credibility: caricatures of working-class people, or upper-class lords and ladies, of detectives and policemen, or of Nazis or Communists or Americans, are all too common. The dramatist's need to amuse, to clarify or to symbolize may wholly deprive a character of reality, and this can happen even to an astute playwright like T. S. Eliot, some of whose representative characters in the naturalistic setting of *The Cocktail Party* barely struggle into theatrical life.

Our discussion of character began on a cautionary note, and it must end on another. The difficulty of assessing the value of a character lies in the multiplicity of his qualities and of his tasks in the play. In the past, as, with some few exceptions, in the present too, the need for a protagonist, a hero upon whom the spectator could focus his attention and who could in himself embrace much of the meaning of the play, encouraged the creation of a stage being rather larger than life, one for whom the other characters were merely foils. But in being created a protagonist with a set of personal relationships, such a character must, under the hand of an artist, take on something of a life of his own. In *Hamlet* there seems at first glance to be a simple pattern of characters, with the hero the dominating one on whom all others reflect light, his strength emphasized by their limitations: (i) in the diagram below. In fact, each particular relationship, of Hamlet with his mother, or with his father's ghost, and so on, illuminates unique facets of his ambiguous position. He grows in complexity as a result of each exchange. In the end, the personality we think of as Hamlet is better suggested as a cluster of reactions, becoming increasingly complicated as the play progresses: (ii) in the diagram.

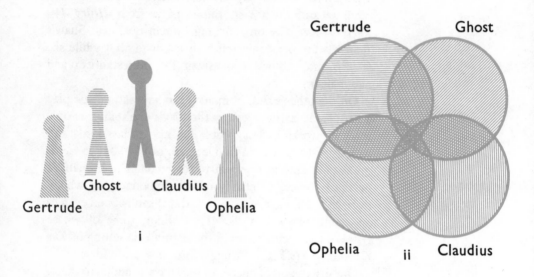

Thus, in his formation, a character may take on vitality and even seem to 'develop', as Hamlet seems to grow more circumspect in seeking his revenge, more intricate and more self-conscious, or as Lear seems to change from proud king to humble beggar and then finally to find his place as a man. Embodied by an actor in performance, the character will assume an immediacy, appearing to live before our eyes. When this happens, any theorizing about the purely functional attributes of character becomes suspect, and the imaginative interchange between actor and spectator, with all its unpredictable energy, will prevail.

5   What's in a plot?

Plot versus theme

In a good play the events do not matter as much as what they stand for. A *plot* might be roughly described as those events pieced together to make up a story, which may sometimes make sense on its own. It is in this extracted story that we sometimes find interest and excitement in a superficial way; but in doing so we may neglect the play's dramatic theme. A *theme* involves the real purpose for which a play is written, as well as the tenor and meaning pervading the whole. Because drama makes its points only in terms of human behaviour, it must of course use the actions of human beings, but it is usually a mistake to think that these actions are more than a means to a greater end.

In most plays we are compelled to remember the feelings and ideas accentuated by the way the story is treated. It is often this dramatic quality which is under-estimated in reading, but which contributes essentially to the play's meaning in performance: the increasingly bizarre interlacing of the entrances and exits of the lovers in *A Midsummer Night's Dream* as Puck's magic takes hold; the cold and the warmth, the harshness and ease of the costume and décor, movement and grouping implied by the transition from court to forest in *As You Like It*; the contrast of crowd and tent scenes, of the public and the private life, in *Julius Caesar*. It is only in lesser kinds of drama, like the melodramatic thriller or the ridiculous farce or the detective mystery, that a crude curiosity about events and 'what will happen next?' is of any consequence.

Audiences may today have come to believe that plot and events are all important, because they may still be obsessed by the formula of the nineteenth-century 'well-made' play. This type of drama was perfected by Ibsen on the Continent, and exploited in England by a host of lesser dramatists from Pinero and Galsworthy to Noël Coward and J. B. Priestley. In the well-made play a conviction of reality was a prime necessity; characters must seem true and events plausible, and this illusion could be created only if the dramatist followed a firm set of rules specifically designed to capture, sustain and satisfy the spectator's interest. Suspense born of a sly control of the pregnant situation was the playwright's first concern.

Suppose we wished to dramatize the injustice of the law in a well-made play. We might hit upon the story of a forgery of a cheque. It would not long sustain the drama to illustrate *how* the forgery was managed: of more interest would be the causes and results of the crime, and on these we should have to concentrate. Causes would involve some examination of the forger's character, and results would call for comment on the application of the law. So we might arrive at some such pattern as this: an employee forges a cheque—why?—say, to help a young woman— why?—so that she might leave her husband—why?—because he is a bully. The forger must therefore be represented as kindly disposed, if foolhardy. Next, his forgery must be discovered—but should he be charged?—yes, yet was his motive truly reprehensible? Upon release from prison, he will be unable to get further work—would his sentence not therefore be doubly cruel?—how might this point be emphasized?—he must subsequently kill himself, not in remorse but in despair.

It only remains to arrange this questioning material of cause and effect in such a way as to keep the spectator guessing. To do this, we must keep the reasons for the crime hidden until after it has been discovered and the spectator misled as to the character of the criminal. There would be a nice irony in this. The discovery of the crime would then provide an exciting *exposition*, introducing the situation; the reasons for it would make an intriguing *complication*, since no simple solution would present itself;

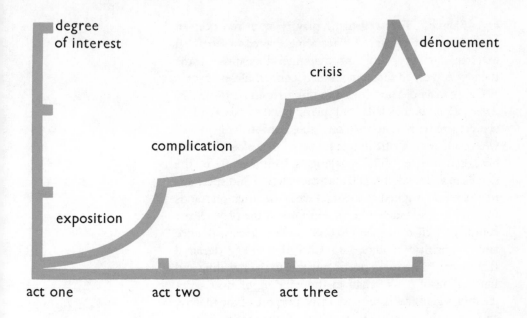

degree
of interest

dénouement

crisis

complication

exposition

act one   act two   act three

The shape of a 'well-made' play

the *crisis* of feeling would follow naturally with the indict-
ment; and the suicide would supply a moving *dénouement*,
or resolution of the events. In this way the well-made
play is built up, and this was the outline of Galsworthy's
clever play *Justice*, which in 1910 contributed to political
thinking on prison reform.

Yet though our interest is certainly sustained in this
play, the genuine quality of that interest is doubtful. We
remain inquisitive eavesdroppers, and in no real sense
undergo the experience ourselves. This, paradoxically, is
because we are too much in sympathy with young Falder,
the clerk who steals the money, and quite opposed to
James How, the merciless employer who charges him.
The simplicity of our response encourages a comfortable
pathos on our part: we tend to sit back luxuriously and

cry, 'Shame!' The well-made play is often too neat an arrangement of events, each act being shaped to satisfy an external curiosity, and not the inner demands of the theme. A painted face can scarcely conceal lifeless eyes.

Galsworthy did not drop into this error in *Strife* or *The Silver Box*, better balanced plays because we tend to sympathize with more than one side, but the danger in all well-made naturalistic drama remains: that plot will be an obsession in itself. The ravelling and unravelling of the details of a lifelike situation may cause writer and spectator to be so short-sighted as to forget what the situation stands for, and to lose touch with the purpose of the play. Shaw compared well-made plays to cats' cradles, clockwork mice and mechanical rabbits, and Christopher Fry declared that there was no more poetic purpose in the ravelling and unravelling of a plot than in the winding of wool. Re-creating a genuine experience is the purpose of the theatre, and when this purpose is lost sight of, the theatre itself is in jeopardy.

Total dramatic experience

To see how minor a part 'plot' plays in creating the real impact of a play, let us look at the means by which Shaw makes his theme felt in the fine second act of *Major Barbara*.

Barbara is a major in the Salvation Army, and she has brought her father Andrew Undershaft, the munitions millionaire, to see the shelter in the East End of London, where she works to help the poor and destitute fight the evils of society. In the first part of the scene she shames Bill Walker, a fearsome Cockney ruffian, who has assaulted Jenny, a young Salvation Army girl. Barbara stands up to him and then refuses the conscience money of a sovereign with which he hopes to be forgiven. Now, full of enthusiasm, Mrs Baines, the Army Commissioner, enters to announce a gift of £5000 from a Lord Saxmundham, on condition that another donor will double the sum. Undershaft offers to do this, but gently points out that Saxmundham is really a whisky distiller whose name was formerly

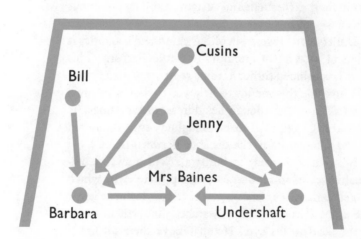

The visual pattern in *Major Barbara*, Act 2

Bodger. Deeply distressed that Mrs Baines can accept soiled money, Barbara indicates that she will leave the Army.

Such is the plot-line, but the meaning of the scene emerges only after we have been made *theatrically* aware of the values placed upon the crucial announcement of the gift: the different reactions to Bodger and what he represents create a dramatic dialectic that pricks us like so many needles.

The contrasts between each of the main characters, their speech and movement, attitude and reaction, suggest an essentially thematic construction of the scene:

1. Mrs Baines displays an over-simple Christian gratitude, reiterated almost comically in ecstatic cries like, 'My prayers have been answered', 'Heaven has found the way'. She is echoed innocently by Jenny with 'How blessed, how glorious it all is!' These two hold the centre of the stage while the ironic comments of the others fly about their heads.

2. Barbara's initial response to the news is joyful, but as she digests its true meaning, she draws apart from the others in their excitement and sustains a still and ominous silence.

3. Undershaft's revelation of Saxmundham's identity is the first of a series of attempts to nettle Barbara. This manner is continued through ironic remarks to Mrs Baines like, 'I give you this money to help you to hasten my own commercial ruin'. Although he addresses Mrs Baines, he is diametrically opposed to his daughter, and we should sense the antagonism in the distance between them.

4. Bill's sarcastic aside to Barbara, 'Wot prawce selvytion nah?' serves to remind us of the principles by which she acted earlier, the very ones which now torment her.

5. Cusins, Barbara's fiancé, watches the scene of battle with the devil in his eye. He sits above them all like a cynical puppet-master, our representative on the stage, mocking both Undershaft and the Salvation Army. He echoes Mrs Baines and Jenny, and starts, then swells, the noise of ironic rejoicing—until in a sudden decisive moment of quiet we hear Barbara's stricken, low-pitched refusal.

Here is Shaw pressing his meaning home, forcing Barbara to question herself, and the spectator to judge the values of realist and idealist. And all this is preparatory to the irresistible challenge of Undershaft's model city in

Act III, where Barbara's brother Stephen's forthright but naïve statement, 'Right is right; and wrong is wrong . . . that's all', is confounded. It is not in plotting that Shaw here controls his theme, but

1. *Verbally*, in the contrasting words and tones given to Mrs Baines, Undershaft and Cusins: sentimental, ironical and cynical (though Shaw does not place as much weight on the verbal element as many critics think).

2. *Visually*, in the stage picture which reflects first the separation of Barbara from Mrs Baines, and then the conflict of father and daughter. The ingenuous Mrs Baines is caught between them, while Cusins remains jubilantly aloof.

3. *Musically*, in the control of pace evident in the speeches, building to the climax of Cusins's drum *obbligato*, 'Rum tum ti tum tum . . .' and the anticlimax of Barbara's tormented response, 'I can't come'.

4. *In mood*, by setting Barbara's near-tragic experience in a context of comic, even farcical, dramatic behaviour, forcing the audience to criticize her as well as sympathize with her.

5. *Dialectically*, in marshalling the clashing attitudes of the characters: romantic, realistic; spiritual, cynical; passionate, indifferent.

These are some of the ways by which a play's theme is illuminated, and this analysis suggests craftsmanship of another order from that of Shaw's contemporary, John Galsworthy, one which makes a 'What's next?' curiosity largely irrelevant. The statement, question, comment and mood of the play are communicated by all the elements of drama.

When a play is written in this way, exploiting all our dramatic faculties, events as such fade into insignificance. Indeed, in some plays events have little impact at any level, as in conversation pieces like Congreve's *The Way of the World* and Shaw's *The Apple Cart*; in some they hardly bear more consideration than melodramatic swashbuckling, as in Marlowe's *Tamburlaine* and Shakespeare's *Macbeth*, or than the incredibilities of farce, as in *A*

Midsummer Night's Dream and Synge's *The Playboy of the Western World*; in some the events are so domestic as to be of little account in themselves, as in *Othello* and Sheridan's *The School for Scandal*; and in some modern plays there may be no events at all, as in Dylan Thomas's *Under Milk Wood* and Samuel Beckett's *Waiting for Godot*.

Therefore we look beyond plot for the dramatic experience as a whole, which is something that cannot be predigested as a story. This is one reason why we can never say precisely what a good dramatist is 'saying', since such an experience cannot be summarized in so many words. A play exists in the form it takes in order to compel us to encounter the author's motives, ideas and feelings in writing the play.

For the most part, a play's theme is marked by *the ordering and emphasis of its parts*: by the balance of characters, by the choice of its poetic imagery, by changes of mood and tone, by the arrangement of scenes. In this again there is no law, only the law of each play unto itself.

True dramatic structure

The extraction of a plot from a play often gives a false idea, too, of its true shape and structure. Even a simple story, like that of *Romeo and Juliet* or Shaw's *Pygmalion*, may reveal a more complicated shape and image in performance.

When Shakespeare hit upon Arthur Brooke's poem, *The Tragicall Historye of Romeus and Iuliet*, as material for dramatizing, it would have been a straightforward decision to counterpoint the lyrical scenes of ideal love with the cruel and violent ones of the Montague-Capulet civil faction. His alternation of these scenes would certainly torment us with a lively image of ill-fated lovers, but melodramatically. Yet a greater power in the play arises from his unpredictable use of the worldly Nurse for Juliet, and the brilliant introduction of a cynical Mercutio as confidant to Romeo. The impact of the play comes, not from a sharply contrasted beauty and ugliness, or good and evil, but from a more complex interplay of feelings, some

intensely involved, others amusedly detached. Laughter provides a buffer for the crude opposition of love and hate.

To take a modern example of a deceptive structure: the plot of *Pygmalion* seems to spring from the myth of Galatea, the statue brought to life by Venus, and this might well have suggested a dramatic form to the playwright. But Shaw ensures that his play does not offer the

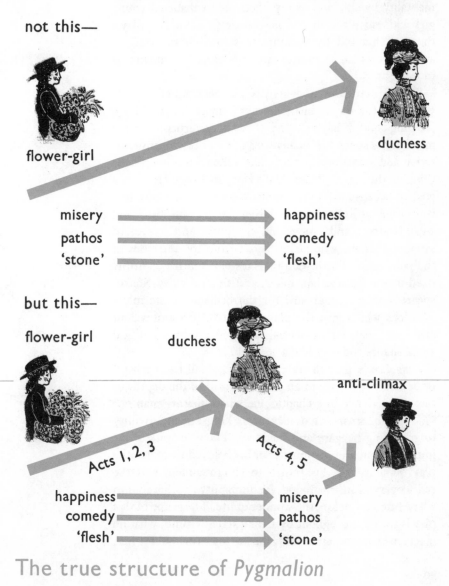

The true structure of *Pygmalion*

easy satisfaction of a 'Cinderella' story, one of a poor flower girl who becomes a duchess, or of a stone Galatea who is granted the fullness of life by having her social status raised. On the contrary, after leading us foolishly to believe that Professor Higgins's task is finished when Eliza has deceived the nobility at the ball, Shaw abruptly changes the mood of the play. He explodes our sentimentality by showing us a pathetic and exhausted young girl with no place in her new society. Thus the play's theme is marked by a complete structural reversal, an anticlimax which at once disappoints us and stimulates us to thought.

The structure of a good play is determined by the vitality of the theme in the author's imagination. Like a growing child, it has a quality of constant surprise. In the mind of the spectator it conveys a sense of bright improvisation and yet of inevitability, like a living and not a dead thing on the stage. Prince Hal's story in *Henry IV, Part I* is alive because he is the dramatic centre of the carefully contrasted attitudes of his father Henry, his firebrand rival Hotspur and, above all, his gross and irreverent satellite Falstaff, who stands apart from the intrigues of the politicians. The legend of Hal's gay youth was firmly fixed in the Elizabethan mind, and this provided Shakespeare with a springboard for the brilliant comic interpolations which give the play its delightfully ambivalent character. Falstaff's essential sanity in a grimly political arena shapes the play like a see-saw.

King Lear's pattern traces the King's fall from power, pride and confidence in an orderly world to the depths of bitter experience in a chaotic one where neither man nor God may be trusted; a descent from kingship and divinity to grovelling beggary and madness. Then, in spite of his imprisonment and the murder of his beloved Cordelia, the play demonstrates his return to enlightenment and the rediscovery of his manhood, his humanity and his soul in a new humility before the wonder of life. The shape of this play is traced throughout by Lear's state of mind, what he meets in character and event, the setting provided for him

KING

Prison   Court

DIVINITY

humility   tyranny

discord

harmony

Hovel   Heath

ANIMALITY

madness   storm & chaos

BEGGAR

The structure of *King Lear*: 'I am bound / Upon a wheel of fire'

and the shifts of feeling in the poetic imagery. Shakespeare designs a perfect pattern to suit the needs of his immense theme, a pattern which conveys a sense of man's revolving on fortune's wheel.

Subplots

The approach to a play as a total experience makes it difficult to accept that such a thing as a subplot exists, as if it were possible to detach one from its main plot and arrive at two short plays instead of one long one. A subplot is nothing if it does not make an integral contribution to the communication of the theme. The story of Falstaff is in no real sense a subplot of the story of the Prince, any more than the story of Enobarbus's loyalty is separable from that of Antony's duty in *Antony and Cleopatra*. In *The School for Scandal* Charles Surface's sincerity and success are inseparable from his brother Joseph's hypocrisy and failure. Nor can Miss Prism and her hand-bag be detached from their context in *The Importance of Being Earnest*.

At most it is merely a convenience to talk of 'the Gloucester subplot' in *King Lear*, for this play above all demonstrates an absolute unity of plot and subplot, in structure and in feeling.

The many points of comparison and contrast between Lear and Gloucester have frequently been made. In A. C. Bradley's view, for example, they are both old, white-haired widowers; they are both wounded by the child they favour hastily, and healed by the child they wrong. They both suffer through their own folly, but learn their lesson in the end, echoing each other's thoughts about 'poor naked wretches', and so on. In the structure of the plot, the development of the one is accurately linked with the development of the other: Gloucester's concern for the King enables Edmund to destroy his father, and Edmund's new authority causes those who destroy the King, Goneril and Regan, to bring ruin upon themselves. In this the play is plotted with a juggler's dexterity.

Yet Shakespeare's greater effort is directed towards placing these two pathetic figures side by side in our minds, so that the one measures the stature of the other. The physical and particular suffering of Gloucester seen out of its context would horrify the most hardened theatre audience, but Shakespeare sets the gruesome scene in which Gloucester's eyes are gouged out immediately after the pitiless scene of the mad Lear holding grotesque court in the hovel. This orchestration of effects serves both to diminish the importance and mere sensation of blood-spilling, and to increase our sense of Lear's mental agony. Thus both scenes have *an equal role to play* within the act, which is indivisible and continuous. Indeed, in one sense, we may feel that this sequence of scenes is itself a subplot of those Gods who are invoked throughout the play. In this way the play broadens and expands to embrace the nature of life, and Gloucester's pain and Lear's agonized misery become symbolic of the suffering of all mankind.

Planes of action and related devices

Subplotting at its best is therefore a way of promoting the theme of the play, and in *King Lear* the apparently simple story of Gloucester in fact encourages us to respond more and more profoundly as the action proceeds. The orchestration of the tragedy controls our response at all levels, and the elements of this orchestration must include the development of character, the symbolism of character, the running verbal debate on the divine reason for evil in nature, the guiding emphasis of the poetic imagery, and the pattern of the action as a whole. This pattern takes us from the discord of a tyrannous court to the greater discord of the storm in man and nature, and on finally to the pity and simplicity of Lear's reconciliation with his good angel Cordelia.

In the Play (Meaning)	Level	In the Audience (Response)
a domestic quarrel of family and state	PLOT AND NARRATIVE	interest at surface
Lear's growth of understanding	PSYCHOLOGICAL	we analyse and share his suffering
a recognition of good and evil	MORALITY	we are teased by allegory
a debate on God and the problem of suffering	PHILOSOPHICAL	we are teased by dialectic
a dirge on man's ambiguity as animal and angel	POETIC	we feel through the rhythms and imagery
the place of man in the universe resolved	DRAMATIC PATTERN	we respond to the whole experience

Levels of meaning and response in *King Lear*

Contrasted kinds of mood and style, character and action, may also contribute to our impression of a play. Although Falstaff does not speak to Henry IV, it is not enough to discuss Shakespeare's view of the King without his view of Falstaff. The Porter does not address Macbeth, but on a comic plane his remarks are entirely relevant to Macbeth. Comedy may not seem to sit well with tragedy, but Shakespeare never hesitates to introduce the one into the other. By this technique he acknowledges that the true action of drama is not simply that of the presentation of events on the stage, but rather the creation in our minds of the links between one character and another, between one speech and another, and between one scene and another. The idea or 'image' of the play is built up *in the imagination of the spectator*: it is we who set Falstaff beside the King, and apply the Porter's words to Macbeth. We must defer to Dryden's definition of action: 'Every alteration or crossing of a design, every new-sprung passion or turn of it, is a part of the action, and much the noblest,

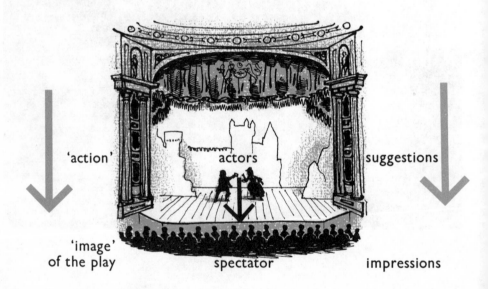

'action'   actors   suggestions

'image'
of the play   spectator   impressions

The true action of a play is in our minds

except we conceive nothing to be action till the players come to blows.' The image of the play can be most alive when the stage is quite still.

Only if we acknowledge this can we appreciate the delicious complexity of, for example, Shakespearian comedy. In the fantasy world of these plays Shakespeare can most readily orchestrate not only subplots but also different *planes of action*. In *A Midsummer Night's Dream* we look through the sane eyes of Theseus and Hippolyta, as it were, at the fanciful interchange of the romantic lovers, and at the hilarious burlesque of love in the scene of 'Pyramus and Thisbe'; and through the mischievous eyes of Puck we see the delicate fairy world of Titania shivered by the broad comedy of the clowns, in particular in the person of the irrepressible Bottom.

Sometimes it is Puck who makes this interplay possible, sometimes the juxtaposing of characters and scenes, and at one time it is done by the device of the play-within-the-play which Philostrate organizes as Master of the Revels. But at all times we link the different sets of players imaginatively in order to arrive at the play's 'meaning'.

The careful reader will be able to apply this principle of dramatic 'orchestration' to other plays created with a poetic imagination, like *As You Like It* and *Twelfth Night*.

As You Like It makes itself felt through another masterly pattern of comic contrasts: courtiers are mingled with true lovers, shepherds with clowns, fools with philosophers. Shakespeare's abiding interest in bringing together incongruous figures, manners and moods is given full scope by the device of placing the court in the countryside, and releasing our fancy in the forest. He can rebuke the whimsical pastoral lover Silvius with the sensible old rustic Corin, the infatuated Orlando with a teasing Rosalind, the sophisticated wit Touchstone with his delightfully undignified Audrey, while Rosalind herself presides over all with her gentle realism and pretty sincerity. The passage from the tyranny of the court is a dramatic leap into an apparent chaos of contradictions in human attitudes to love and life.

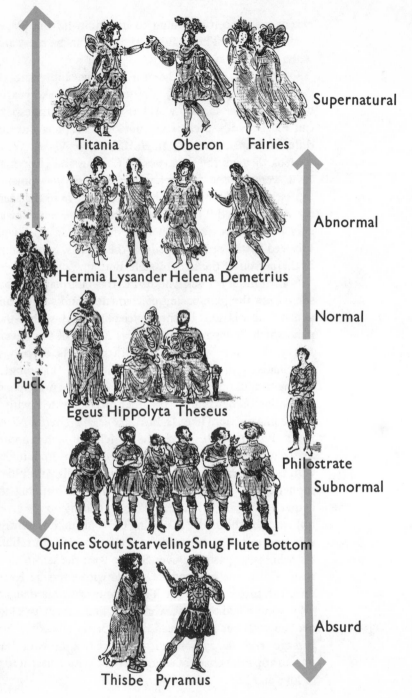

Titania   Oberon   Fairies   Supernatural

Abnormal

Hermia Lysander Helena Demetrius

Normal

Puck

Egeus Hippolyta Theseus

Philostrate

Subnormal

Quince Stout Starveling Snug Flute Bottom

Absurd

Thisbe   Pyramus

Planes of action in *A Midsummer Night's Dream*

Twelfth Night has an equally ingenious design, the earnest and genuine Viola balancing the self-centred Orsino and Olivia, and a worldly Sir Toby balancing the self-deluding Malvolio and the vain and vacant Sir Andrew. In the sparkling central scene of the play (3. iv), Shakespeare contrives to bring the earnestness and mockery into sharp conflict, the romantic Olivia embarrassed by the clumsy Malvolio, and Viola herself by, of all people, the featherweight clown Sir Andrew. The structure of this scene, a scene of rapid changes in plotting, character, tempo and mood, is worth a study on its own. It bears comparison with the splendid scene of the sheep-shearing feast in *The Winter's Tale* (4. iv), in which pastoral comedy slips into homely farce, and the romantic into the tragic.

This balancing of characters and scenes especially applies to tragicomedy. Shakespeare's increasing sense of the moral contradictions of life led him to attempt a balance of tragic and comic mood, and of the sincere and the cynical tone. The inadequate laws of man bring into question the unfathomable laws of God, and Shakespeare expressed his unease by writing human tragicomedies like the outstanding *Measure for Measure*. In this 'problem' comedy, Isabella is a novice who attempts to intercede for the life of her brother Claudio, condemned to death for seduction. His judge, Angelo, is attracted by Isabella's beauty and shows himself as weak as the man he has condemned so severely: he will only pardon Claudio if Isabella will submit to him. By all the antitheses of this stark plot, Shakespeare is able to set one urgent idea against another, until the spectator is forced to re-examine his position: is Isabella's virtue worth more than Claudio's life?

The shape of this play encourages our sense of weighing one set of moral values against another, while, with an amoral glee, characters like Lucio and Pompey persist in kicking at the finely balanced scales.

Thus a simple analysis into exposition, complication, crisis and *dénouement* will not always do justice to plays of this calibre, plays which exploit different planes of action and mood. T. S. Eliot is another dramatist who determines the structure of responses to his drama by a variety of contrasts, sometimes in his poetic imagery, sometimes in the form of his verse, sometimes in the attitudes of his characters. *Murder in the Cathedral* contrasts the thoughts of Thomas à Becket with those of the Knights who come to kill him in the King's name, and both are set against the feelings of the common people, as represented by the Women of Canterbury. *The Cocktail Party* contrasts the greater destiny of Celia Coplestone with the lives of the more mundane Edward and Lavinia.

Eliot's *The Family Reunion* provides a useful illustration from the modern field. In this play we are made to feel that the hero, Harry, Lord Monchensey, is a vital character. Because he speaks a more profound and subtle language, we place him high on the scale of sensibility that the variety of the verse proposes, and the mood of the play is varied according to the intensity of the poetry. Harry's feeling is so strongly contrasted with the trivial minds of most of his family that violent ironies are created:

Poetic	level:	Harry Agatha
Scale of sensibility		Amy
Prosaic	level: Ivy	Violet Gerald Charles

Ironies in *The Family Reunion*

Harry wrestles to comprehend his own soul, trying to discover why he wished to push his young wife overboard, and to understand what is haunting him in the family home of Wishwood. But he discovers, and we feel, that neither his mother Amy nor the comic chorus of uncles and aunts can begin to see his problem. Amy herself rules the family in her effort to re-possess him, and rages against her sister Agatha, who can better understand him and in some degree share his mental burden. The play is a structure of distinctions and contradistinctions of sensibility and understanding, pursuing a mood of discord which only ends in harmony with the revelation of the truth of Harry's past.

The manipulation of interest and the Unities

It would be fair to say that the dramatist tries to capture our interest in his theme, not always by an exciting story, but as often as not by carefully arranged *contrasts*. Contrast is the essence of good drama.

Liveliness on the stage comes with the contrast of character with character, tone with tone, scene with scene, and so on. It is contrast which helps us measure one person or feeling or idea against another. It is also contrast which catches our attention: the activity that ensures our constant interest is that in which we are continually being asked to judge each *ironic* effect or impression in relation to others that have gone before. It is the ironic placing of Lear beside his Bedlam beggar that gives a sharp meaning to the scene on the heath; it is a revelation of Macbeth's weakness to juxtapose him with a wife of such apparent strength of will. Plays which introduce ironic contrasts satisfy a deeper interest and intensify their drama.

It is no coincidence that the plays which create a structure of contrasts and which demand an analysis in depth are 'poetic dramas', if not in their use of verse, in their spirit and intention. For although nearly every play must control the spectator's interest by particular events presented, complicated, brought to a head and finally resolved, the impulse thrusting it into a special shape and giving it a special energy is determined by the unpredictable law of an intense imagination. Like a good car, a good play matches the shape of the vehicle to the power of the engine.

Happily, an audience can sense this quality of artistic life, and, given the occasion, an audience's imagination, like its interest, will readily grow and proliferate as a living thing. The theatre, a palace of the imagination, provides that occasion.

In presenting his theme, a good playwright will instinctively use this capacity of an audience, and will pose problems of feeling, thought and behaviour that demand to be answered. Samuel Beckett's *Waiting for Godot* is a play with no plot in the usual sense, a play in which the characters remain at the end as they were at the beginning. But it is compulsive because it captures the imagination: certainly the spectator is not unchanged when the curtain falls. A play proceeds by persisting with 'questions', which it forces us to put to ourselves and which grow more pressing and incisive during the performance. Then it may choose to answer them or not: a play which makes no attempt to supply the answers can be a fully satisfying experience. A complete statement of a problem, even an insoluble one, can have *an imaginative unity*.

It is now possible to see in better perspective the three dramatic 'Unities', of action, place and time, which were attributed to Aristotle, the Greek philosopher who first tried to analyse drama as early as the fourth century B.C. The unity of action, and what Aristotle meant by this, is still arguable: the unities of place and time, which Aristotle discussed but never proposed as a law, have now become largely irrelevant.

That a play should be assumed to happen in one place and last for no more than twenty-four hours are laws which can restrict the presentation of many themes, and may bear little relation to the manipulation of interest. Where they have existed in some degree, as in Greek tragedy and the French classical tragedy of Corneille and Racine, they have been a temporary matter of convention rather than essential rules. Dr Johnson neatly exploded the idea of the unities of place and time by reminding us that the spectator is always aware that 'the stage is only a stage, and that the players are only players'. This is only partly true—our flight into an imaginative other world does take place. Moreover, the unity of time may recommend itself in a tragedy which begins at the point of crisis in order to generate that shocking quality of inevitability we find particularly in Sophocles and Ibsen. But plays like *Macbeth*, *Henry V*, *Antony and Cleopatra* and *The Winter's Tale*, each of which ranges between two countries and over many years, convey a strict sense of their unity because it is the pressure of the theme that dictates the form of the drama.

The unity of action proposes that a play should have a single plot. The concentration of attention which is implied by this unity is clearly of great force in tightly organized plays like Sophocles's *Oedipus the King* and Shakespeare's *Othello*. Yet it is possible to maintain that attention is no less concentrated in *King Lear* with its subplot, or *A Midsummer Night's Dream* with its contrasts of kinds of character, or *Measure for Measure* with its mixture of levity and seriousness. The true unity of action is the unity possible to the imagination, and this is probably what Aristotle meant when he suggested that a play must represent a complete whole in which the incidents are so closely connected that the transposal or withdrawal of any one of them would dislocate it.

The mind has the power to reduce to unity a multitude of impressions, and to fuse apparently discordant elements in the intense heat of a great dramatic experience. Of this Shakespeare's drama offers proof enough. If we can ever fully answer the question 'What's in a plot?' we shall have found the key to all that is incalculable in great drama.

6   Comedy, tragedy and the mood of the audience

Kinds of drama

When we go to a play, we begin to learn from many details what *mood* the play is to be in: from the bill which announces 'an uproarious comedy' or 'a thrilling drama', from a musical overture perhaps, from the colour and style of the setting, from the tone of voice of the players, from the speed of their playing. We quickly adjust ourselves to the appropriate frame of mind, and throughout the performance the play directs our reactions. Because of the compressed form of drama, few dramatists let their audience flounder for long in uncertainty: the time available for building a response is too valuable. When, however, we have only the book to read, the burden of supplying the right mood and atmosphere falls on us.

Of all the problems of silent interpretation, this is the least easy. Without the style and tone of an actor with a stage presence, the heightened speech of tragedy can fall flat. Reading the disembodied words of Shakespeare's clowns without the funny face and gait of the comic actor, without his careful timing and pointing of jokes by voice and gesture, is like trying to enjoy a good meal by poring over a cookery book. What is worse, there are so many gradations between broad farce and high tragedy, even within the same play, that the precise mood the playwright intends at any one time may elude us.

Yet it *is* possible to recognize this mood in reading, although we have only the words to work with. There is

a noticeable difference of tone between the sound, rhythm and imagery of

If music be the food of love, play on (*Twelfth Night*)

and

>When shall we three meet again
>In thunder, lightning, or in rain? (*Macbeth*);

or, in the question and answer of dialogue, between the polished wit of a servant replying to his master,

Did you hear what I was playing, Lane?
I didn't think it polite to listen, sir. (*The Importance of Being Earnest*)

and the edginess of the soldiers who say,

>Who's there?
>Nay, answer me; stand and unfold yourself. (*Hamlet*)

It is essential by such hints to recognize the kind of play being read. The playwright's signals begin at the beginning.

The difference between tragedy and comedy is at bottom, therefore, one of mood, and their conventions of style have grown up in the service of that mood. At one time, comedy's traditional ending was the happy one of a marriage contracted, celebrated or implied. It has often been remarked that a wedding in real life is only the beginning of another drama, but here was a quick, easy and acceptable way of ending on a joyful note. Even though Claudio of *Much Ado About Nothing* or Bertram of *All's Well That Ends Well* or Angelo of *Measure for Measure* deserved no such respectable departure from the scene, the mood demanded it; some comedies, like *As You Like It* and *Twelfth Night*, conclude with a positive orgy of simultaneous betrothals. By convention, too, the all-or-nothing catastrophe of high tragedy demanded the death of the hero, death suggesting the extremity of sorrow and a unique finality. But there is no doubt that death for a Macbeth or an Othello in real life would have been a happy release, and that the melancholy present at the end of plays like *Troilus and Cressida*, *The Misanthrope*, *The Cherry Orchard*, *The Playboy of the Western World*,

Juno and the Paycock and *Waiting for Godot* arises from the sensation of life having to go on. Nevertheless, the ritual and symbolic element in death transfigures the endings of *Romeo and Juliet*, *Hamlet* and *Antony and Cleopatra*.

However, we are not so concerned in this chapter with the outward signs of tragedy and comedy as with the qualities in them that create their characteristic mood. There are broad differences of feeling, obviously. Tragedy tends to exalt man as an individual, by exploring his place in a world inhabited by fateful forces, and by showing how important he can be in the face of insuperable odds. Comedy tends to see man as a social animal, and to belittle his dignity by making him one of a crowd. Tragedy tends to punish man with a punishment out of all proportion to his sin, but only after making us feel that he is being crucified for sins that are ours too. Comedy gently mocks him for his ultimate unimportance, but only after we have shared a little of his humiliation. Tragedy encourages us to be passionate; comedy usually seeks to bring the intellect into play—Horace Walpole's dictum comes to mind: 'Life is a comedy to the man who thinks, and a tragedy to the man who feels.'

Nevertheless, it is a travesty to imagine that there is no thought in tragedy and no feeling in comedy. The whole question is fraught with contradictions. Many of Shakespeare's plays share the qualities of both tragedy and comedy, and for plays of modern times the use of such labels as tragedy and comedy is a questionable practice.

Comedy, farce and burlesque

The characteristic mood of comedy causes a pricking of the mind, and it may sometimes, though not necessarily, express itself in the physical noise of laughter. Yet the simple definition of comedy as 'a play which produces laughter' is unhelpful. There are so many degrees and kinds of laughter, from the horse-laugh to the reluctant smile. There are so many uses to which comedy can be put, from satirical social criticism to the quiet illumination of some intimate aspect of life. There are so many methods of creating it, from the coarse antics of a circus clown to the smooth wit of a well-turned vocal inflexion. There are so many standards by which it can be judged, the standards of Aristophanes, Shakespeare, Molière, Shaw, the great comedians of Western drama, each of whom is different in temperament and purpose, and whose audience differed in character and background. Moreover, the texture and tone of the greatest comedy is so finely balanced that every new actor or reader may tip the play into either the pathetic or the ridiculous.

Certain recurring elements are nevertheless found in comedy in small and large proportions, and of these two may be reasonably identified:

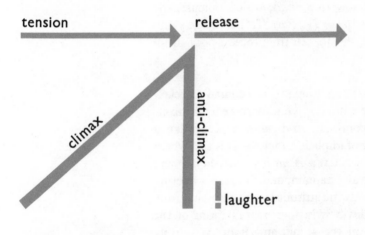

Anticlimax

1. *A relaxing of tension,* which indeed is characteristic of all kinds of humour. Consider the nonsense joke which the psychologist Freud has analysed: 'Never to be born were the best for mortal man. But hardly one man in a hundred thousand has this luck.' The tone is at first

serious and the words appear to be moving to a dignified conclusion. In the issue, the illogic of the statement belies this tone: we break into laughter, by which we show that we refuse to believe. Humour which contains a germ of wisdom operates in essentially the same way, like Oscar Wilde's joke in *Lady Windermere's Fan*: 'In this world there are only two tragedies. One is not getting what one wants, and the other is getting it.'

The two essentials for relaxing tension are:

(i) tension in the first place, helped by the actor's straight face, or his serious delivery of the words (this is especially important in a farce); and

(ii) a ludicrous anti-climax, involving a loss of dignity and a consequent release of feeling.

Even a pun works in this way, where we supply a second and unexpected meaning to a word, which ridicules the first. Says Falstaff in *Henry IV*, *Part II*, 'Discharge yourself of our company, Pistol.' In the process, poor Pistol is mocked.

2. *Incongruity*. Just as a dramatist can contrive a relaxing of tension, so he can contrive a more general incongruity which may continue throughout a scene like a running commentary of implicit criticism. It is this which runs through most of Shaw's *Arms and the Man*, where Sergius, a gallant cavalry captain, and Raina, his adoring lady, represent the romantic attitude to war and soldiering. But Bluntschli, a realistic Swiss mercenary fighting on the other side, appears on the scene, and Raina is warmly mocked by finding herself in sympathy with the enemy in spite of herself. In Act 2 the whole business of being a noble lady arming her lord for the fight—at one point Sergius declaims, 'I have gone through the war like a knight in a tournament with his lady looking down at him!'—is ridiculed by Raina's urgent need to conceal her unpatriotic adventure with Bluntschli in Act 1. Her pretence falsifies every fine sentiment uttered, and a delightfully two-faced comedy, with the spectator well in the secret, is the result.

The incongruity of comedy often depends on the exaggeration of a character or a situation, an excessively fat Falstaff or foppish Malvolio, or *A Midsummer Night's Dream* situation where everyone falls in and out of love too easily, so that we immediately contrast our own *normality*. We laugh, but only perhaps to realize that the object of ridicule was no different in kind, only in degree, from ourselves or our own behaviour.

Henry IV, Part II offers some of the best comic scenes in Shakespeare, and an analysis of 3. ii reveals some of his great range of comedy, as well as some of his many methods of creating anticlimax and incongruity. The opening exchange between Shallow and Silence, two senile gentlemen chatting about their happy youth, is inimitable. Silence, the quieter of the two, prompts Shallow, the more voluble, to retell the tales they have obviously heard many times over. They chuckle and nod pathetically at the feeble jokes they hold in common: 'You were call'd Lusty Shallow then, cousin,' says Silence, and the spectator contrasts the vision of a young gallant with old Shallow as he is now. These two are quite innocent of the incongruous figures they are cutting, and are absolutely serious about themselves. But at the same time, their dialogue provides an accurate insight into the minds of people growing old, and, in spite of its fun, it is full of warmth and human understanding. The two old men can accept the approach of death, and yet still keep a weather eye open for the market prices. This is a true example of *humorous comedy*, in purpose ultimately compassionate.

The entrance of Bardolph of the red nose and pimply face introduces a *farcical comedy* of another order. The following scene in which Falstaff examines the forced recruits from the unsophisticated countryside of Elizabethan Gloucestershire displays a collection of clowns: the shaking Mouldy—'a good-limb'd fellow', says Shallow; the excessively skinny Shadow, who declares himself to be 'his mother's son'; the ragged Wart, whose 'whole frame stands upon pins'; the burly Bullcalf with his assumed cough, 'caught with ringing in the King's affairs,

upon his Coronation-day, sir'; and above all the tiny portrait of bravado in enthusiastic little Feeble, 'I can do my
good will, sir, you can have no more.' Although this scene
makes a sly comment on the injustice of conscription in
Elizabethan times, this is broad, farcical material offering
an opportunity for verbal wit of no great consequence, and
for a good deal of comic stage business, which cannot fail.

When, to escape the recruitment, Bullcalf and Mouldy
finally resort to bribing Bardolph, their 'good Master
Corporal Captain', the tone changes more to that of
satirical comedy. Falstaff's recruiting campaign no doubt
had already some satirical edge; now that he accepts the
bribes, the corruption of those in authority, Falstaff and
Shallow, is under fire. Justice Shallow is a prize himself:
'If the young dace,' croaks Falstaff, referring to himself,
'be a bait for the old pike, I see no reason, in the Law of

Nature, but I may snap at him'—it is natural for dog to bite dog.

The laughter of comedy can be cruel or kind, satirical or sympathetic, and we must beware of expecting the same effects from every comic play. The table below attempts to distinguish some different kinds of comedy.

Genre	Object	Method	Ironic tone	Examples
humorous comedy	to understand and reveal human nature	observation of behaviour, with balanced criticism	gentle, sympathetic, compassionate	Shakespeare, Sheridan, Synge, Fry, Dylan Thomas
satirical comedy	to correct manners, morals and ideas	exaggeration of faults, with dramatic wit or sarcasm	objective, rational, mocking	Ben Jonson, Congreve, Shaw, O'Casey
farcical comedy	to ridicule life, but only for laughter	invention of absurd situation, exaggeration of character	light, amoral, cynical, indifferent	(elements in) Goldsmith, Wilde, Pinero
burlesque	to ridicule other drama	caricature of characters, and parody of language	light, critical, often sarcastic	*A Midsummer Night's Dream*, Act 5, *Knight of the Burning Pestle, The Critic*, Acts 2 and 3

Table of comic forms

Where comedy with its laughter stimulates thought and directly criticizes characters, manners and ideas current at the time, it can be as serious as tragedy. It is a mistake to regard, say, *As You Like It* as a lesser play than its contemporary *Julius Caesar* because the former deals with social behaviour by the methods of comedy and the latter deals with political behaviour by those of tragedy. Both can affect us profoundly, and comedy, which can give us a glimpse of ourselves when we are least on guard, may have claims to being a more valuable and dangerous weapon of attack.

Farce is the kind of comedy which causes little more than a 'physical' laughter, and the mind has nothing to do except register a rapid series of wild incongruities of behaviour. The typical farce of Victorian and modern times is so broad that humorous insight or satirical point can be missing. As in the comedy of mistaken identity in Roman times, and in the *commedia dell'arte* of sixteenth- and seventeenth-century Italy and France, the characters are clowns and puppets; the situations of comic intrigue and error are fantastically complicated and improbable. However, even in a farcical context it is sometimes possible to recognize a more purposeful humour at work.

Wilde's *The Importance of Being Earnest* is largely farcical, but the scene at the end of Act 2, in which Jack and Algernon quarrel over their broken engagements, offers a fair sample of Wilde's mixture of purpose:

JACK. I wanted to be engaged to Gwendolen, that is all. I love her.

ALGERNON. Well, I simply wanted to be engaged to Cecily. I adore her.

JACK. There is certainly no chance of your marrying Miss Cardew.

ALGERNON. I don't think there is much likelihood, Jack, of you and Miss Fairfax being united.

JACK. Well, that is no business of yours.

ALGERNON. If it was my business, I wouldn't talk about it. (*Begins to eat muffins.*) It is very vulgar to talk about one's business. Only people like stockbrokers do that, and then merely at dinner parties.

JACK. How you can sit there, calmly eating muffins when we are in this horrible trouble, I can't make out. You seem to me to be perfectly heartless.

ALGERNON. Well, I can't eat muffins in an agitated manner. The butter would probably get on my cuffs.

The puppetry of the characters, their echoing each other's phrases, the stiffness of their gestures, the rapid pace of the dialogue, and above all the explosion of the quarrel into terms of eating or not eating muffins—all this bears the hall-mark of traditional farce. But, meaningless in themselves, their words do identify Jack and Algernon as two well-bred young gentlemen who seem to consider eating muffins as important as breaking an engagement, and who, beneath the restraint of their decorum, have bad tempers like other mortals. Thus Wilde slyly insinuates his comment on the fashionable young men of his time.

Some elements of dramatic burlesque may often be found in all kinds of drama: Silvius and Phoebe in *As You Like It* are borrowed from pastoral comedy; the Knights in *Murder in the Cathedral* and the Chorus in *The Family Reunion* speak like the well-bred automata of English drawing-room comedy. But burlesque proper is today found only in sophisticated revues, and full-scale burlesque dramas were more common in the seventeenth and eighteenth centuries, when the circle of people who went to the theatre was small, compact and self-conscious about its theatre-going. This points to a prerequisite of burlesque: that the spectator must be as familiar with the kind of drama being burlesqued as the author himself. However, the mockery of Pyramus and Thisbe in *A Midsummer Night's Dream*, Act 5, or of heroic tragedy in Sheridan's *The Critic*, Acts 2 and 3, is so general in its effect as to be thoroughly enjoyable even to a modern audience. *The Critic* draws mercilessly upon all the styles and conventions of speech and action of its originals: exposition in which two speakers tell each other what they already know, the confidante who echoes grotesquely every mood of the heroine, the soliloquy spoken at all costs, the asides which follow upon one another to exhaustion, and so on. By his first act Sheridan extends his play to include a brilliant criticism of current attitudes in the theatrical world as a whole.

Tragedy and melodrama

Some of the most exciting and uplifting drama the theatre has known has been tragedy, in spite of the disaster and tears with which we usually associate it. Its grand and unaccountable effect upon the spectator has made it the most discussed kind of drama and the most difficult to analyse. Neither philosophers, psychologists nor literary critics have been able to touch the mystery at its heart, and the evidence of every reader and spectator is equally valid in the task of searching it out. It is the special response great tragedy achieves, however, which seems almost impossible to re-create in this century, and these two problems, what tragedy does to the spectator and why it is missing today, are bound together, as we shall see.

This is not the place to recount the arguments that have surrounded Aristotle's original bold assessment of the effect of tragedy, that it should 'purge' us of our emotions by pity and fear, but simply to indicate that there is an ideal and an actual response to a great play like *Hamlet* or *King Lear*. It is one thing to assert that one is intended to respond with pity and fear, and quite another to analyse one's actual feelings in performance. For the reader in the cool detachment of his room, a tragic response is something he will have to conjure from an already overworked imagination, if he can.

An estimate of the *quantity* of emotion a tragedy may arouse must be some measure of its worth, but only if we also estimate its *quality*. An unrestrained gush of feeling is as meaningless as a pot of paint thrown at a wall; but feeling which is controlled by the thought it stimulates offers a meaningful and unforgettable experience. Aristotle's suggestion that the tragic response was a *catharsis*, an emptying of emotion, can therefore be misleading, but his notion of a unique conjunction of the painful feelings of pity and fear is a useful starting-point for the discussion of a tragedy.

The spectator's *pity* alone is not difficult to prompt: if a hero is placed in a situation where he may be destroyed, a simple sense of possible loss may be enough to wring tears of sentiment from an audience. These are cheap tears, cheaply won, and such a play is written to secure emotional sensation. Emotional drama of this kind was common in Shakespeare's time, and so-called 'tragi-comedies' like Beaumont and Fletcher's *Philaster* have never been absent from the English stage.

To this sort of play the name *melodrama* has clung since later Victorian times when it won a great popularity. *The Lancashire Lass, or Tempted, Tried and True*; *Pure as Driven Snow, or Tempted in Vain*; *Faithful until Peril, or*

a Father's Dishonour and a Daughter's Shame—such is a fair sample of the titles by which these plays were advertised, and in each it was sensationalism providing the advertisement. Virtuous characters, sweet and innocent girls and bold and frank-faced young men, confront imminent danger to life and honour, but courage and virtue prevail; the happy ending was an additional sop to the audience. It was a spectacular drama, overacted in the manner of the time, its morals absolutely proper, although sometimes the subjects titillated where they should have condemned: altogether its dramatic experience was artistically dead. Much that is seen on popular cinema and television today remains of this kind, although we owe to Ibsen the reintroduction into European drama of socially real and honest subjects. With Ibsen and his successors serious drama became adult again, and pity was used more sparingly.

Fear, too, is a stirring emotion on its own, and in a barbaric age is easy to achieve, as the theatre at the decline of the Roman Empire proved. Dramatic entertainment which resulted in the actual death of the performer introduced a sensationalism rare in history. For obvious reasons this form has not survived into modern times, but in any case it could not have created true tragedy.

Yet fear which stirs us to a strong response can be most valuable for drama, if it is used to make us understand the nature of life; fear of God, of society or of our own weakness can do this. Pity, the feeling by which we can share, in common humanity, the sufferings of others, can also be an emotion of dramatic value. An artistic conjunction of these two feelings, the one inviting us to share the sufferings of a character, and the other warning us to avoid his mistakes, can shock us into immense imaginative activity. By it we can re-create a human experience within ourselves and receive a tremendous illumination of what man is and is not, can and cannot do. Although we are in a theatre, this can be a first-hand experience in that this controlled pain leaves a feeling of exultation and an understanding of being alive.

A poetic style, whether of Elizabethan blank verse or of Sean O'Casey's poetic prose, must obviously help this mood, but it is only likely to arise if three essential tragic elements are present:

1. *A hero* of some stature. The spectator must have a strong, but human, focal point for his sympathy. If the hero is petty, he risks ridicule, and the play may slip into nondescript tragicomedy. Although a hero who invites laughter may not destroy our sense of his universal significance, the ingredient of laughter begins to counteract the power of our fear for him: Dr Faustus's use of Mephistopheles's gift for scenes of pure farce dangerously undermines our concern for his fate.

2. *An outcome felt to be necessary and probable*, that is, in the given circumstances of the hero's situation, we must feel that the events at the end of the play must always or usually take place. If we suspect that they are *improbable or impossible*, that they could occur only occasionally or never at all, the drama will sink into melodrama or even burlesque. This *inevitability* in the situation and its result is only likely if we feel that forces beyond the hero's control are present in the play.

The force present in the play	*Examples*
the gods, the devil	Zeus in Aeschylus's *Agamemnon* Mephistopheles in *Dr Faustus* the Gods in *King Lear*
the supernatural	the curse on Sophocles's Oedipus the Soothsayer in *Julius Caesar* the witches in *Macbeth*
fate, chance, fortune	the enmity of the houses in *Romeo and Juliet* the unidentifiable power of Godot
the power of heredity and nature	the sea and the past in Synge's *Riders to the Sea* inherited sin in *The Family Reunion*
immoderate weakness, ineffable passion	the love of Antony and Cleopatra, Naisi and Deirdre the jealousy of Othello the sensuality of the Duchess of Malfi

The inevitability of tragedy

So-called 'tragic irony' arises because we are aware of the irresistible nature of these forces, while the hero is not. They are indeed the cause of our pity and fear, and the modern French dramatist Jean Cocteau went so far as to describe tragedy as a spring which will slowly unwind the whole length of a human life, being all part of a machine perfectly built by the infernal gods for the mathematical destruction of a mortal. At the moment when the hero *recognizes* the irresistible power of this machine of destiny, either his soul may be delivered like Lear's, or his mind shattered like Othello's.

3. *A shared belief in the audience* that there is a moral law in the universe which will translate senseless evil and misery into significant experience. They must sense a reason and purpose in suffering, though its mystery may never be fully understood. A wholly unreasonable world, where death is arbitrary and life a gamble, would again reduce tragedy to melodrama. In such a world pure chance may bring pain, but chance may equally relieve it. On the other hand, a Christian tragedy is a contradiction in terms: the deaths of Milton's Samson or Eliot's Becket lack tragic tension because their souls will have certain salvation. Great tragedy, in other words, must force us to feel the values by which man lives his life, and if we cannot easily share with the writer his evaluation of human worth, as tends to happen in Eliot's *The Cocktail Party* and in the existentialist drama of Jean-Paul Sartre, the drama may fall from tragedy to propaganda.

The change in the nature of tragedy from Greek to modern times can be partly explained by the loss of such communal values. The Greeks practised a highly ritualistic tragedy, the function of the hero and the shape of the play falling into a set pattern, and to disrupt this was to defy the expectations of an audience attending a religious function and commit a kind of sacrilege. Even the stories of the Greek tragedies were well known to the spectator, so that the dramatist dare not, and did not want to, do more than re-interpret familiar material by placing fresh emphasis upon it in different ways; when we know a story well, even a slight change in its events or tone of telling can suddenly capture our intense interest. We can never fully know the religious experience of Greek tragedy again, simply because we cannot satisfactorily re-create the role of a Greek audience.

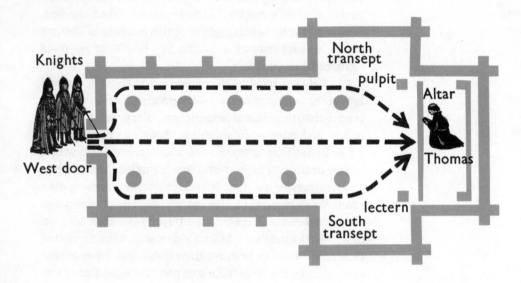

Church as theatre

A successful attempt to reintroduce a ritualistic form into drama was T. S. Eliot's *Murder in the Cathedral*, where elements familiar to a Christian audience ensured an unprecedented degree of success for this kind of play. The audience knew the Becket story; the writing and presentation echoed elements of the church service; soliloquy could be introduced in the form of the Christmas sermon; some of the verse could take on the incantatory rhythms of the church litany; the choir could function as a dramatic chorus, and the congregation as an audience.

The whole church became a ritualistic theatre with the chancel as its chief acting area. By such means the ceremonial of the drama acquired a meaning greater than itself, but this is not an experiment easily repeated. Christopher Fry's daring play about man's violence towards man, *A Sleep of Prisoners*, did not make a ritualistic use of the church building as an acting arena, and perhaps took our knowledge of the Bible too much for granted. In an age of doubt such a play may only be able to achieve a partial success.

The source of tragic vitality in Elizabethan times was the force of the audience's sheer wonder at the immensity and the ambiguities of life. When a Renaissance man could at the same time be a courtier and a statesman, command a ship and an army, play an instrument and write poetry, when a gentleman could cultivate the art of living and retain an intense curiosity about his immortal soul, the theatre turned the spotlight from God on to man himself. Every great tragedy of Elizabethan times was an experiment in dramatizing and making trial of the possibilities of man's nature. A nobility and a robustness characterized the best of Shakespeare as he sought to press into dramatic form his questions about good and evil, order and disorder, love and hate, the beautiful and the ugly. His sense of the quality of life and its passing grew more acute, and the presence of death in life increasingly supplied the essential element of tragic fate. From *Romeo and Juliet* to *Antony and Cleopatra* and *Coriolanus* he explored the personality of man and the forces at work upon him from without and within. Even the uninhibited Jacobean tragedians of blood and horror, like Webster, Middleton and Tourneur, through the macabre illuminate the quality of living. Grotesque effects in which a mother is given the wax corpses of her children, or a corpse with poisoned lips is dressed and painted as a beautiful girl, can in their context intensify the final enigma of death.

The *heroic tragedy* of the Restoration and the years that followed, of which Dryden's *All for Love* is the best-known example, seems to substitute a make-shift and over-pathetic tragedy, drawn without real reference to the life of the time, for the true experience. Love and honour replace the notions of suffering, questioning and defiance; sentiment replaces feeling; rhetoric replaces poetry; a superman replaces a human hero. A self-conscious society audience permitted social comedy, but it constricted and flattened the huge impulse of tragedy. *All for Love* makes better sense than its romantic model *Antony and Cleopatra*, but the mystery at the root of such a character conception as Shakespeare's Cleopatra, a symbolic queen but a realistic woman, and at the root of the contest between the world and the spirit in Antony, shows Dryden's tragedy to be comparatively shallow. In the nineteenth century the domesticating of potentially heroic situations by more naturalistic treatment virtually prohibited tragedy in the total meaning of the term.

Tragicomedy and problem drama

The idea of *comic relief*, which introduces laughter into a context of intense feeling, suggests that a whole range of mood is possible for an audience within one play. Yet while it is easy to release the tension built up by tragedy, it is not so easy to make the resulting laughter relevant to the tragic theme. Where it is used with an instinctive perception of the audience's response, as with Lear's Fool, Macbeth's Porter or Hamlet's Polonius or his Gravedigger, comic 'relief' is something of a misnomer. Since it is known that the Gravedigger is joking over the very grave into which Ophelia is shortly to be lowered, and since the Fool's comments on Lear's plight accurately point the tragedy, to force laughter upon the audience in this way is to twist the knife in the wound. Shakespeare in these plays achieves a *unity of feeling* in spite of the mixture of moods and the incongruity of the parts.

Outside tragedy proper, the history of English drama from the Mystery Plays and the Elizabethan dramatists onwards shows that dramatists are aware of the dramatic interest in mixing the dominant moods of comedy and tragedy, although something that is neither comic nor tragic is the result. Shakespeare, the greatest experimenter of all, achieved a wholly original effect by introducing Falstaff and the tavern scenes, the unheroic side of life, into his *Henry IV* plays; and in his 'problem comedies', *Troilus and Cressida*, *All's Well That Ends Well* and *Measure for Measure*, potentially tragic subjects like the destruction of love by war, the conflict of reason and passion, and of love and honour, are treated with apparent levity: a sour taste is left in the mouth, but a stimulating argument in the mind. These plays, too, succeed in creating a unity of feeling. By insisting that the spectator see the matter from another point of view, compelling him, as it were, to stand back and review his feelings, Shakespeare amazingly anticipates the tone of much twentieth-century drama, for which the critical term 'alienation', that is, of the audience, has recently been adopted.

Today we deal no longer in tragedy, it seems, but in problem plays, propaganda plays, modern morality plays, plays of ideas, or simply 'dramas', and we are at a loss to explain our response to them as either tragedy or comedy. With the movement for naturalistic drama, dramatists imposed upon themselves the limitation of being as like life as possible, and refused themselves the heightening of tragedy and the exaggerations of comedy. Those who came very close to reproducing the true sensation of living, like Ibsen and Chekhov on the Continent and Synge and O'Casey in Ireland, quickly discovered that tragedy and comedy were two sides of the same coin, and the naturalistic theatre aimed more and more to thrust together the laughter and tears in indivisible mixtures. Such plays allow us a degree of emotional response, while at the same time they keep us critically alert, and the inadequate term 'tragicomedy' is the only one we have to describe them.

Synge's masterpiece, *The Playboy of the Western World*, satirically tells the story of Christy Mahon, a farm lad on the remote west coast of Ireland. Christy thinks he has killed his father in a fit of temper, and runs away to seek refuge in a distant inn. There he discovers to his great astonishment and delight that his deed is regarded as courageous, and his defiance of the law as heroic. His strange acquisition of fame is treated by the playwright with a keenly comic eye, but the tone abruptly changes when those at the inn find that Christy's father is not dead after all. Mahon makes a dramatic appearance and the villagers begin to punish Christy viciously for having deceived them. In an irresistible last act the comedy becomes bitter and the mood sharply realistic and intensely thought-provoking.

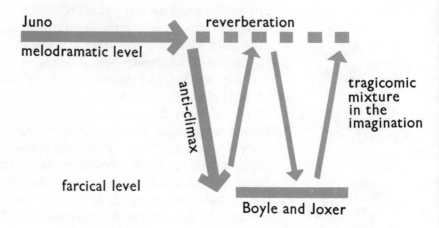

Ironic contrast in *Juno and the Paycock*

O'Casey's *Juno and the Paycock* would have been a stark portrait of a Dublin family caught in the net of poverty, misery and the Irish Rebellion. The play is ennobled by the presence of a monumental heroine, Juno, the mother whose faith in God and life survives a series of personal misfortunes. But her husband, Captain Jack Boyle, who struts through the play and through life like a 'paycock', together with his boon companion, a lovable lay-about named Joxer Daly, transform the mood by their ludicrous presence. They constantly deflate the melodramatic and assert the farcical tone, until we are left with a complexity of feelings, ones that are balanced and sane, yet passionate and unfathomable.

The play ends on two notes: first with Juno's highly emotional, incantatory lines,

Sacred heart o' Jesus, take away our hearts o' stone, and give us hearts o' flesh! Take away this murdherin' hate, an' give us Thine own eternal love!

and then with the drunken entrance of Joxer and Boyle. Joxer sings,

Put all your throubles in your oul' kit-bag, an' smile, smile, smile!

and Boyle philosophizes tipsily,

I'm telling you . . . Joxer . . . th' whole worl's . . . in a terr . . . ible state o' . . . chassis!

To discover the mood of this play, it is no help to refer to its label, 'A Tragedy in Three Acts'; we must consult our own hearts and minds. *Juno and the Paycock* remains a kind of play different from tragedy or comedy because of the mingling of contradictions in the imagination.

The simple logic of traditional comedy and the coherence of tragic feeling have on the whole been rejected by twentieth-century drama. In our time the meaning of life is not explicit and its plot is obscure. An absolute tragedy or comedy depends upon a confidence in moral or social values, and the predominance of tragicomedy today suggests that our values are uncertain and shifting.

7   Drama in its medium

In the cinema

The special opportunities and limitations of the medium
in which a play is to reach its audience may decisively alter
its character. This fact is especially important today when
we are as likely to find it in the cinema, on the radio or on
television as on the stage. The extraordinary expansion of
the media for drama in the twentieth century makes it
imperative to know what harm, if any, may be done to a
play written for a medium other than the one being used.
Have we seen Shakespeare's *Hamlet* when we have seen
Sir Laurence Olivier's film?

The cinema, which has set out to dazzle its audience in
a competitive world of entertainment, seems to have the
power to do anything a dramatist might ask. Ernest
Lindgren concludes his very useful introductory book,
The Art of the Film, with the words: 'Is it possible to
conceive of any impression which the eye might behold
or the ear hear, in actuality or in imagination, which could
not be represented in the medium of the film? From the
poles to the equator, from the Grand Canyon to the
minutest flaw in a piece of steel, from the whistling flight
of a bullet to the slow growth of a flower, from the flicker
of thought across an almost impassive face to the frenzied
ravings of a madman, is there any point in space, any
degree of magnitude or any speed of movement within the
apprehension of man which is also not within the reach of
the film?'

This is impressive indeed. Nevertheless, we must
answer the question whether there is anything the film
cannot do, by declaring firmly, 'Yes, there is.' *Ideas and*

feelings present as difficult a problem of communication in the cinema as they do in any other medium.

Any art is to be judged by its means of emphasis, as poetry by its power over words and their associations, music by its rhythm and melody. Therefore film cannot be considered only as a succession of photographs, however marvellous. If it could, the cinema would never have developed from its childish beginnings: in 1898 fascinated audiences watched the miracle of 'no less than three express trains' rushing through a railway cutting; today they watch the highly complex drama of Shakespeare or Shaw.

The film's means of emphasis resolve themselves into three:

1. *The size of the image,* and especially the cinema's power to show great detail in close-up. Among the details a dramatist might wish us to see clearly and emphatically are the actor's eyes and mouth; and often his hands and feet too may vividly express some aspect of his character and situation.

Long shot

Medium shot

Close up

The size of the screen image

2. *The movement of the camera*, the artificial eye that directs and controls our attention. It may descend into a house or into a crowd, finally coming to rest upon the object or person of dramatic interest; it may 'pan' or 'track' along a line of faces to note their expressions, as in the play-scene in Olivier's film of *Hamlet* or at the coronation in his *Richard III*; it may look down upon a victim or up at a bully, and in this way help us to capture the feeling in the situation.

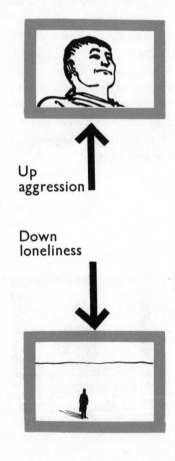

Up aggression

Down loneliness

Camera angle

3. *The 'editing' of the pictures*, by which one length of film is cut at a specific point and joined to another. By rapid 'cutting' the pace of a fight or an argument can be enlivened; or we can be made to associate one idea with another, as when the famous Russian director Pudovkin alternated an actor's face with an inviting bowl of soup and convinced the audience that the man was hungry. An average feature film can have well over 1,000 such cuts.

All of these powerful directives to the imagination can be hackneyed, and have been many times. A close-up of a kiss is used to suggest love, or of a tear-stained cheek to suggest grief; cheap technique here replaces careful analysis. Alternate cutting between crooks and policemen suggests the excitement of a chase. But a good film will use these effects delicately, since their visual impact is so strong that it may swamp any precision of meaning in the dialogue. Loose thinking and emotional blur are the cinema's greatest danger.

A real trial of the film's power of communication is the filming of Shakespeare. This has been attempted many times in the short history of the cinema, but only with rare success in short sequences. Film would seem well fitted to interpret plays written for the freedom of an unlocalized stage; the close-up might seem to be the natural equivalent of the soliloquy, always difficult to convey from within the proscenium arch; the movement in depth possible on the Elizabethan stage finds an echo in the camera's unrestricted tracking; and Shakespeare's rapid sequence of scenes might seem to be the equivalent of the free cutting of the film.

But Shakespeare's is verse drama, and his poetic images are created to release the imagination; whereas the visuals of the film must always be as particular and limiting as a photograph. In Olivier's *Hamlet* we see the sea of troubles from the impressive height of the castle of Elsinore, but the camera cannot show us the slings and arrows of outrageous fortune: the mind is not left to assimilate this poetic image, but is bemused by other startling shots while it is being spoken. What do we remember from

Olivier's *Henry V*? The brilliant reconstruction of the Globe theatre, the glorious cavalry charge at Agincourt, the flight of the English arrows. What do we remember from his film of *Richard III*? The stifling of the Princes, the hunchback's shadow falling across Anne's white dress, Clarence drowned gruesomely in a wine-vat, the Duke of Norfolk falling to his death in full armour. Yet not one of these exciting visual effects is properly in Shakespeare at all.

In George Hoellering's film of T. S. Eliot's *Murder in the Cathedral*, the restless camera of this photographic and naturalistic medium found itself at a loss during Becket's long speeches, and it roamed irrelevantly over the stained glass and other features of the church. The Women of Canterbury could hardly sustain the artificial convention of an impersonal chorus at close quarters, and were treated as individual actresses showing us aspects of medieval home life.

The experience of poetic drama tends to be dissipated in the cinema because the film asks for the restrained acting and speaking of extremely naturalistic drama. The dialogue is, however, written for projecting across an auditorium, and its language is often highly conventional. It is almost impossible to be naturalistic, as the film directors Joseph Mankiewicz with *Julius Caesar* and Renato Castellani with *Romeo and Juliet* tried to be, when the words are in verse. The treatment of soliloquy in the cinema is a crucial problem: Olivier has shown us a motionless face while we listen to the voice on the sound-track; Orson Welles has shown us emotive pictures of thunderclouds moving across the sky while we hear his voice say, 'Tomorrow and tomorrow and tomorrow.' Only once has a soliloquy truly succeeded in the cinema, when Richard III's frank confession that he was 'determined to prove a villain' (I. i) was spoken by Olivier directly to us from the screen. Here the bold breaking of the cinema's convention, combined with the peculiar nature of this soliloquy, created some of the startling impact we imagine the original to have had.

Shakespeare on the screen is thus a test case. Olivier attempts an intelligent compromise between the ways of the stage and the ways of the cinema; the result is neither good theatre nor good cinema. Orson Welles makes 'a film on a theme by Shakespeare', and creates a creditable film which is unrecognizable Shakespeare. Which is better? Perhaps to see effective cinema, to see Welles's huge, gnarled hand held close to the lens, reflecting Macbeth's impassioned lines,

> Will all great Neptune's ocean wash this blood
> Clean from my hand?

Perhaps not. The film has an enormous power of *synthesis*, bringing together and building up emotional impressions, but a limited power of *analysis*, breaking them down and examining them. This hardly suits the more complicated and precise verbal communication of impressions characteristic of good drama. For this reason one must watch a film of a play aware of what it can do and what it cannot.

The true art of the film at its greatest lies quite outside the literary sphere, and under the hand of a brilliant director it has the power to focus a merciless and subtle eye upon the actuality of life. There is another dimension of drama in Chaplin's comic-pathetic portraits of poverty and injustice, in the simple understanding of Flaherty's documentaries of primitive life, in the immense, yet lyrical and satirical, world of Eisenstein, in De Sica's exquisite and compassionate studies of Italian working-class life. In a truly international art, the triumphant personal vision of men like the Japanese Kurosawa, the Swede Ingmar Bergman, the Indian Satyajit Ray, and many others, has greatly enriched the visual poetry of the film since the war. But this is the subject of another study.

Radio drama

Plays on the wireless had a difficult beginning: it was hard to imagine that a play, which had always been associated with something *seen*, could ever be anything but a poor second best when it was only *heard*. But of all the new dramatic media, only radio has fully evolved its own dramatic form, and in Louis MacNeice's *The Dark Tower*, Dylan Thomas's *Under Milk Wood* and Samuel Beckett's *All That Fall* it may claim to have created great drama in its own right.

Again, however, it is important to recognize the limitations of radio. To conceal microphones on the stage and then perform the play as for a spectator with his eyes open to signals belonging to mime and gesture, is to make nonsense of plays written for the theatre. From the silent approach of the unseen eavesdropper to the grand entrance of the central figure, from the conflict of carefully composed groups in Shakespeare to the intruder creeping through a darkened room and concealing papers in his pocket in modern melodrama, visual action stands to lose too much of its point.

However, radio has two great features which distinguish it from the theatre, features which are assets in the creation of another kind of drama:

1. *It is blind.* It therefore has the power to release the tremendous energy of the imagination, which was characteristic of the bare stage of the Greeks and the Elizabethans. It is therefore a 'poetic' medium: music, sounds, voices, words, anything that might encourage the imagination into activity, may make it flower abundantly. Indeed, the listener's imagination may rapidly run riot, and the sound of a seagull or a cow can waft him with the speed of thought to any beach or farm of his choice. It was noticeable that Douglas Cleverdon, the producer of the B.B.C.'s notable performance of *Under Milk Wood* (available on Argo's record RG 21–22), refused to mix music with Thomas's evocative poetry, lest the one overwhelmed the other. This freedom to make imaginative leaps from place to place at the suggestion of a sound, or to leap forward or backward in time, encourages the success of dream plays and fantasies, and the three plays named above are of this kind.

2. *It is intimate.* The listener is isolated from his fellows, and he feels that the voice in the loud-speaker is speaking to him alone. It was this which made Hitler, a platform

orator, a poor broadcaster, while Roosevelt had the 'microphone manner'. It is this which makes 'habit' listening possible, and why homely programmes and panel games continue regularly for years. For drama, the soliloquy, the intimate voice in the private ear of the listener, is as natural to radio as it was to the Elizabethan stage; the chorus, completely disembodied, returns as a dramatic force; and the idea of a narrator, borrowed from the novel, is completely acceptable, and makes the adaptation of novels for radio an easier task than it might have been.

Under Milk Wood employs two narrators who lead us gently into the dream world of its Welsh village characters, and Thomas's poetic prose uses a graphic imagery and rhythm to fill out our mind's picture of a scene:

Time passes. Listen. Time passes. Come closer now. Only you can hear the houses sleeping in the streets in the slow deep salt and silent black, bandaged night. . . . Only you can hear and see, behind the eyes of the sleepers, the movements and countries and mazes and colours and dismays and rainbows and tunes and wishes and flight and fall and despairs and big seas of their dreams.

Such narrators can punctuate the speech of the actors, pointing a line or remarking a character, and so guiding us towards the precise response of feeling the author wants.

This play breaks all the likely rules for radio drama. Because the ear cannot distinguish between more than a few voices at a time, the vocal casting of such plays as Shakespeare's is difficult for the radio producer; Thomas offers a cast of sixty-nine characters, and yet we assimilate them all without their voices being caricatured. He establishes each one with a few vivid strokes, and they grow familiar as the play progresses. Instead of a simple line of events, a unity of action necessary to avoid confusing the listener, Thomas boldly introduces a whole cluster of little situations arising in the village; yet a dramatic centre exists in its strong sense of community. Radio drama had earlier broken through the three-act tradition, since on the air to 'bring down the curtain' was to lose concentration of interest; but Thomas runs many fragments of scene together with every confidence that the village cycle of twenty-four hours will create a unity of the host of impressions, and suggest the life of the village rolling on and on. Echoing Shakespeare's multiplicity of scenes of alternating moods, or the novelist D. H. Lawrence's structure of emotive episodes, a new structure for the radio play emerges.

In radio drama, variety of tempo becomes a real force, because of the pace at which speech impressions can be received. Differences in tone and colour of voice call for a special technique of crisp and restrained dramatic speech, and subtle and rapid vocal changes between the comic and the pathetic mood are possible. Above all, words come into their own as never before since Shakespeare's time, and both verbally and structurally the way is open for a true poetic drama of the air.

The television play

Live television drama is still in its infancy, and standards for critical comparison are few. But more and more plays are in demand for this voracious medium, and the public will see more and more of its drama as television. An initial method of assessing this latest dramatic medium is to make some simple comparisons with the media already known.

1. Both the *stage* actor and his live television counterpart must provide a sustained performance. Indeed, the extremely technical conditions of television acting, in which the actor must rush from set to set, move every muscle precisely as planned for the camera and then perhaps

by a contrast
of levels

by isolating
him

Emphasizing a character on the
stage and on television

speak passionately into its dead eye, makes his work difficult and demanding. Thus only for the spectator is this a point of possible likeness between the theatre and television, although some theatrical rules are to be roughly transferred to television: those for an effective stage entrance (Malvolio in his nightshirt surprising Sir Toby's drinking party in *Twelfth Night*) and for stressing a dominant character (Brutus or Antony in the Capitol in *Julius Caesar*, or Prospero making magic on his island in *The Tempest*).

The differences, however, are great. They arise from the loss of acting space in the television frame. The eye of the camera may look closely at one thing and one thing only: in the theatre the eye of the spectator can take in a complexity of impressions in an instant. Shakespeare's crowded battle and court scenes have little effect on television; and when Shaw's Saint Joan enters the Dauphin's court, the camera has to select from the multiple reactions of the lords and ladies, while Joan herself is in danger of being forgotten. Grand drama on the scale of Euripides's *The Trojan Women* is dwarfed to petty domesticity; and families like those in Chekhov's plays tend to lose their quality of being complete groups as the camera shifts unhappily from one centre of interest to another. The 'sardine' drama of television lacks the spacial, visual vigour of the stage.

2. Television's apparent likeness to the *film* is misleading. The size of the television screen is relatively the same as that of the cinema in relation to the spectator, but the poverty of definition in the television picture at its present stage of development requires it to use the close-up to such an extent that it loses the electric force of the cinema's more sparing use of this device. With too many close-ups, movement across the screen must be slow, and the bunching of actors prohibits theatrical movement and gesture. The space around a character on the stage or cinema screen lends him interest and individuality, but this must be secured by other means on television. Above all, the limited number of cameras in use at one time restricts the quantity of live cutting that can be done on television, and little of the film's vivid editing is possible; the ratio of cuts in a film to those in a television play is roughly 10 to 1, which suggests that the strength of television does not lie in its visual excitement, but elsewhere.

3. Television shares with *radio* the quality of intimacy, but not of imagination. Television space tends to be photographic, and limited to the actual size of the setting; in television, dramatic time tends to be equivalent to actual time: the imagination can only range as far as the actuality of the play allows. Thus the unreality of both fantasy and farce seems inappropriate to the medium. However, like the radio, it is an intimate medium, and the actor in close-up speaks for the individual viewer. Like the radio, panel games and repetitive family drama are natural to it, and small, domestic subjects, which could carry no weight in the theatre, suit it best. This intimacy encourages a crisp dialogue and a rapid development of the action. There is another quality which television shares with radio: immediacy. This lends a topical, urgent, realistic and almost 'documentary' feel to television drama

at its best, and encourages dramatized investigations into social questions of the moment which result in 'slice-of-life' plays of the extreme kind.

It is fairly easy to deduce from these comparisons what will go well on television. Plays with few characters and no crowd scenes, plays with completely naturalistic dialogue and an unambitious, naturalistic treatment of life make successful television. Studies of human nature in its detailed behaviour in limited situations; tiny vignettes of people living together in untheatrical circumstances; domestic relationships of husband and wife, mother and son, sister and brother; familiar circumstances involving workmates and school-friends, office affairs and street encounters; occasionally events in more emphatic, but essentially lifelike, settings like those of a police station or a court-room—these comprise the restrained, if restricted, world of television drama.

What plays, then, will be likely to suffer from adaptation to television? The extravagant drama of the Elizabethans must lose its theatrical quality on the small screen, as must the stylized drama of Molière, the Restoration, and of Goldsmith and Sheridan. Shakespeare's naturalistic moments can profit from television, and by curtailing the decorative business which commonly dogs Shakespearian stage production, by running scene upon scene and sustaining a dramatic pace, television may be an asset to some aspects of his work; but Shakespeare does not call for naturalistic acting consistently, and his drama never wastes the dynamic space of his great platform for long. On the other hand, plays built up of intense duologues, like some of those of Ibsen, Shaw and Galsworthy, may be more at home with this, the most intimate theatre yet devised.

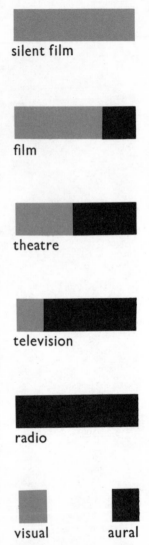

silent film

film

theatre

television

radio

visual   aural

An estimate of the aural / visual strength of the different dramatic media

	FILM	RADIO	TELEVISION
THE SCRIPT			
plot and theme			
characters			
dialogue			
structural awareness of the medium			
visual imagination		n.a.	
aural imagination			
intimacy			
immediacy			
DIRECTION/PRODUCTION			
acting / speaking			
setting		n.a.	
camera: angle, movement, composition		n.a.	
editing of sequences / episodes / transitions			
sound and music			
tempo and style of whole			
VALUES			
audience aimed at			
assessment of success			
with chosen audience			
in chosen medium			
in interpretation of the original			

(n.a.=not applicable)

Formula for the practical criticism
of a play performed on one of the mass media

Styles of presentation in the theatre

We return finally to the stage as the primary dramatic medium. From it the vast majority of dramatic ideas have sprung, and it remains largely free from the financial pressures and from the demands of mass audiences which bedevil the other media. It continues to pioneer experiments with convention, with language and with visual symbolism, always attempting to create new artistic experiences and induce new thoughts and feelings in its audiences. The live theatre still tends to be the testing ground for the other media.

Yet not only the dramatist uses the stage to express his views, but all who have a hand in a finished production. The producer and his actors, the scene designer and the electricians, with many other back-stage workers, constantly seek ways to interpret plays new and old, for their own times and in the light of their own understanding. Each regards himself as an artist in dramatic communication, trying to frame the gigantic drama of the Greeks in the theatre he has to use, trying to fit the awkward Greek chorus within the proscenium arch perhaps, looking for new ways of throwing fresh light upon hackneyed scenes from Shakespeare, trying to adjust the Elizabethan soliloquy or the Restoration aside to conditions not intended for them, introducing new conventions of movement or scenic suggestion or lighting emphasis, all with the intention of kindling interest in some aspect of a well-known play.

They have every right to do this, though there are certain bounds over which these artists may stray with risk to the character or quality of the play they are presenting. Thus a beautiful setting for a play like *King Lear*, which asks only for bare simplicity, may cause the audience to shut its ears to the words; or a lush realistic setting for a play like *Antony and Cleopatra*, which expects a swift continuity of scenes, can be a disaster. A period play may obsess the designer, and a riot of colour and stylish costume may falsify the sombre intentions of the original. Shakespeare, not surprisingly, seems to suffer regularly in

THE ABBEY THEATRE

Convention of acting	Décor and setting	Lighting	Type of play
Naturalistic	detailed and true to period: interiors in the proscenium arch will have 'box' set	source of light must be evident: sun, moon, lantern, electric switch, etc.	naturalistic and problem drama: Ibsen, early Shaw, Galsworthy, early O'Casey, etc.
Stylized	simplified to a few expressive features: arches, cut-out tree, etc.: essential properties only: costumes all equally exaggerated in period	source of light not necessarily seen: may be unreal: colour tones to capture the mood of the play	artificial comedy, of humours, manners, farce: Shakespeare's comedy, Jonson, Molière, Congreve, Sheridan, later Shaw, etc.
Abstract	bare, neutral staging with non-representative, 'sculptural' steps, rostra, etc.: costume loosely in period, but in the mood of the play	'theatrical' lighting, unnatural spotlights, dramatic shadows: with use of cyclorama and emotionally toned colour	Greek tragedy, morality drama, Shakespeare's tragedy, modern expressionistic drama, etc.

Table of conventions in décor, setting and lighting

revival for all these reasons. Every play has its proper style, and this must dictate the manner of the speaking, acting, décor, setting and lighting.

Whatever the style of the play's presentation, it must be devised, like the form of the play itself, to concentrate attention upon the essence of the drama. It must point its theme, evoke its mood, and strengthen the stage action, before it excites the spectator in any other way.

Theatre: the great adventure

These notes may have suggested some starting-points for further thinking about the inexhaustible source of interest and pleasure found in drama and the theatre. The study of drama involves the excitement, and yet the discipline, of understanding and interpreting the world's great plays, bringing them alive for oneself. It is an adventure in imaginative reconstruction. The enthusiast will re-create in his imagination the theatre for which the play was first written, the kind of speaking and acting, the style of setting and lighting; he will imagine an audience, perhaps the original audience, and how the play worked upon it; he will conjure up particular moments in the history of the theatre, and re-experience the mood and atmosphere, the thought and feeling on a great theatrical occasion at a time other than his own.

It may be that he will wish to get closer to the dramatic experience itself, using his whole body in the service of his mind. When this happens, he will act, produce or design, and be a member of a team working as one in the service of the dramatist and the theatre, accepting a subordinate role for an end greater than himself. But as was said in the beginning, the reader has only, at the simplest, to rise from his chair for the spirit and magic of the theatre to enfold him; to speak and move the words is to create life, although on the page they may seem dead. Even read aloud, a play can become a living thing of one's own making.

In that a play is always a reflection of its first audience, to act it in whatever unpolished a way is to recall that audience from the dead; in that good drama has a meaning for all time, to bring it alive is to understand the minds and hearts of one's contemporaries. Good drama can offer an unequalled intellectual, moral and emotional adventure, the greater for the more intense level of interest at which it is approached.

Charts of theatrical history

Note:

1   The left-hand columns usually include playwrights and their plays.

2   The right-hand columns usually include theatrical, literary and historical events.

3   The names in capitals at the left of a chart are those commonly used to describe periods and styles of writing, fashion, architecture, etc.

I. AN OVERALL PICTURE

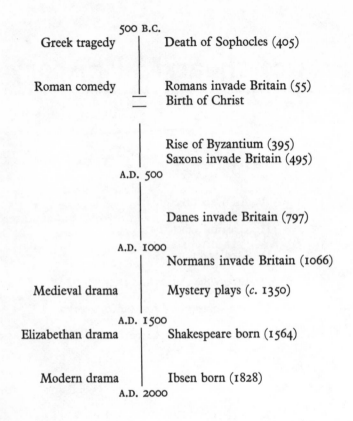

500 B.C.

Greek tragedy | Death of Sophocles (405)

Roman comedy | Romans invade Britain (55)
| Birth of Christ

| Rise of Byzantium (395)
| Saxons invade Britain (495)
A.D. 500

| Danes invade Britain (797)

A.D. 1000
| Normans invade Britain (1066)

Medieval drama | Mystery plays (c. 1350)

A.D. 1500
Elizabethan drama | Shakespeare born (1564)

Modern drama | Ibsen born (1828)
A.D. 2000

GREEK
    (Thespis writing) (*c.* 550)
    Aeschylus (525–456)

500 B.C.

    Sophocles (497–405)
    Euripides (485–406)

    Aeschylus's *Oresteia* (458)
    Aristophanes (*c.* 448–380)
    Euripides's *Medea* (431)
    Sophocles's *Oedipus* (*c.* 425)
    Euripides's *Trojan Women* (415)
    Aristophanes's *Frogs* (405)

400 B.C.

    Menander (343–292)

300 B.C.

ROMAN
    Plautus (*c.* 254–184)

200 B.C.

    Terence (*c.* 195–159)

100 B.C.

    Seneca (4 B.C.–A.D. 65)

First festival of tragedy for Dionysus

First play of Aeschylus (499)
Battle of Marathon (490)
Battle of Salamis (480)
First Greek contest of comedy (459)
                (the 'Old Comedy')
Peloponnesian Wars (431–404)
Pericles died (431)

Death of Socrates (399)
Plato's *Republic* (*c.* 388–347)
Aristotle born (384–322)
Aristotle's *Art of Poetry* (*c.* 334–322)
The 'New Comedy' established (*c.* 330)

Carthaginian Wars begin (264)

Carthage sacked (146)

Julius Caesar (102–44)

Virgil born (70)

Romans invade Britain (55)

Birth of Christ

131

III. MEDIEVAL TIMES

1300

Feast of Corpus Christi ordained (1311)

Dante died (1265–1321)

1350

Mystery Cycles flourished
in Cornwall and at York, Chester,
Wakefield, Coventry, and in
many other towns and cities
(c. 1300–1450)

Langland's *Piers Plowman* (c. 1362)
Petrarch died (1304–74)
Peasants' Revolt (1381)
Chaucer's *Canterbury Tales* (c. 1386)

1400

Battle of Agincourt (1415)

1450

Wars of the Roses (1455–85)
Michelangelo born (1475–1563)
Caxton printing (1476)
Columbus reached America (1498)

TUDOR
John Heywood (1497–1580)
Everyman (anon. c. 1500)
Heywood's *The Four Ps* (c. 1520)

1500

Thersites (anon. c. 1537)

Udall's *Ralph Roister
Doister* (c. 1550)
Gammer Gurton's Needle
(anon. c. 1560)
Norton and Sackville's
Gorboduc (1562)
Preston's *Cambises* (c. 1570)

1550

Elizabeth queen (1558)

Drake's first voyage round the world (1577)
York Plays suppressed (1579)
Star Chamber censorship (1589)

ELIZABETHAN

1570

London's first playhouse (1576)
Holinshed's *Chronicles* (1577)
North's *Plutarch* (1579)

1580 Sidney's *Apology* (1580)

Marlowe's *Tamburlaine* (1587)
Kyd's *Spanish Tragedy* (1589)

Defeat of the Armada (1588)

1590 Spenser's *Fairie Queene* (1590)

Marlowe's *Dr Faustus* (1592)
Shakespeare's *Romeo and Juliet* (1594)
Shakespeare's *Henry IV* (1597)
Jonson's *Everyman in His Humour* (1598)
Dekker's *Shoemakers' Holiday* (1599)

Plague closes theatres (1592–4)
Lord Chamberlain's Company (1594)
Donne writing *Songs and Sonets* (c. 1595)

Globe built (1599)

1600

Shakespeare's *Hamlet* (1601)

Execution of Essex (1601)

JACOBEAN

Heywood's *Woman Killed with Kindness* (1603)
Marston's *Malcontent* (1604)
Jonson's *Volpone* (1606)
Beaumont's *Knight of the Burning Pestle* (1607)
Fletcher's *Faithful Shepherdess* (1609)
Jonson's *Alchemist* (1610)
Shakespeare's *The Tempest* (1611)
Webster's *Duchess of Malfi* (1613)

Elizabeth died, James I king (1603)
King's Company formed (1603)

King's Men at Blackfriars (1608)

1610

Authorized Version of Bible (1611)
Globe burned (1613)
Burbage died (1567–1619)

1620

Burton's *Anatomy of Melancholy* (1621)
Middleton's *Changeling* (1622)
Shakespeare's 1st Folio (1623)

CAROLINE

Massinger's *A New Way to Pay Old Debts* (1625)

James died, Charles I king (1625)
Alleyn died (1566–1626)

1630

Ford's *Broken Heart* (1633)
Milton's *Comus* (1634)
Corneille's *Le Cid* in France (1637)

1640

Civil War, theatres closed (1642)

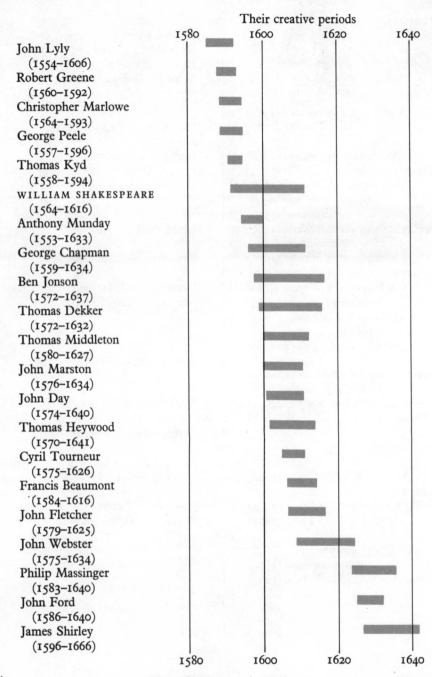

Their creative periods

John Lyly
(1554–1606)
Robert Greene
(1560–1592)
Christopher Marlowe
(1564–1593)
George Peele
(1557–1596)
Thomas Kyd
(1558–1594)
WILLIAM SHAKESPEARE
(1564–1616)
Anthony Munday
(1553–1633)
George Chapman
(1559–1634)
Ben Jonson
(1572–1637)
Thomas Dekker
(1572–1632)
Thomas Middleton
(1580–1627)
John Marston
(1576–1634)
John Day
(1574–1640)
Thomas Heywood
(1570–1641)
Cyril Tourneur
(1575–1626)
Francis Beaumont
(1584–1616)
John Fletcher
(1579–1625)
John Webster
(1575–1634)
Philip Massinger
(1583–1640)
John Ford
(1586–1640)
James Shirley
(1596–1666)

1580   1600   1620   1640

Many dates are conjectural

VI. THE PLAYS OF SHAKESPEARE

Approximate dates	1592	Henry VI, Parts I, II, III
		Richard III
		Titus Andronicus
	1593	The Taming of the Shrew
		The Comedy of Errors
		The Two Gentlemen of Verona
		Love's Labour's Lost
	1594	Romeo and Juliet
	1595	A Midsummer Night's-Dream
		Richard II
	1596	King John
		The Merchant of Venice
	1597	Henry IV, Part I
	1598	Henry IV, Part II
		Much Ado About Nothing
	1599	Henry V
		As You Like It
		Julius Caesar
	1600	The Merry Wives of Windsor
		Troilus and Cressida
	1601	Hamlet
	1602	Twelfth Night
	1603	—
at the Globe	1604	All's Well That Ends Well
		Measure for Measure
		Othello
	1605	—
	1606	Macbeth
		King Lear
	1607	Antony and Cleopatra
		Coriolanus
		Timon of Athens
	1608	Pericles
	1609	—
at the Blackfriars	1610	Cymbeline
	1611	The Winter's Tale
		The Tempest
	1612	—
	1613	Henry VIII

1640

Commonwealth (1642–60): theatres closed
Louis XIV king of France (1643–1715)

1650

Mrs Elizabeth Barry born (1658–1713)

RESTORATION   1660   Restoration of Charles II (1660)
Pepys's *Diary* begins (1660–69)
Patents for King's Theatre (Killigrew) and
      Duke's Theatre (Davenant) (1661)
First Drury Lane (Killigrew) (1663)
Molière's *Misanthrope* in France   Great Plague (1665): theatres closed
(1666)
Racine's *Andromache* in France   Dryden's *Essay of Dramatic Poesie*
(1667)   (1667)
Davenant died (1606–68)

1670

Dryden's *Marriage à la Mode*
(1672)   Wren's Drury Lane (1674) opened
Etherege's *Man of Mode* (1676)
Dryden's *All for Love* (1677)
1680

Otway's *Venice Preserved* (1682)

Otway died (1652–85)
Declaration of Rights (1689)
1690

Etherege died (1635–91)
Lee died (*c.* 1653–92)
Vanbrugh's *Relapse* (1696)   Purcell died (1658–95)
Collier's *Short View* (1698)
Congreve's *Way of the World* (1700) 1700   Dryden died (1631–1700)
QUEEN ANNE   Queen Anne (1702–14)
Farquhar's *Beaux' Stratagem* (1707)   Union of England and Scotland (1707)
Farquhar died (1678–1707)
1710   Betterton died (1638–1710)

1720   Wycherley died (1640–1715)
Vanbrugh died (1664–1726)
Congreve died (1670–1729)
Steele died (1672–1729)
1730

Addison's *Cato* (1713)

GEORGIAN

1710   Handel in London (1710)

George I (1714–27)
Garrick born (1717–79)

1720

George II (1727–60)
Goldsmith born (1728–74)
Gay's *Beggars' Opera* (1728)   Addison died (1672–1729)
Fielding's *Tom Thumb* (1730)   1730

Covent Garden opened (1732)

Carey's *Chrononhotonthologos*
(1734)

Licensing Act to restrict attacks on the
Government (1737)

1740   Cibber's *Apology* (1740)
Garrick's first appearance (1741)

Garrick manages Drury Lane (1747–76)

Johnson's *Irene* (1749)

1750

Sheridan born (1751–1816)

Sarah Siddons born (1755–1831)

1760   George III (1760–1820)
Garrick abolishes audience on stage (1762)
Sadler's Wells opened (1765)
Johnson's *Preface to*   Garrick conceals proscenium lights (1765)
Shakespeare (1765)

1770   Beethoven born (1770–1827)
Goldsmith's *She Stoops to Conquer*
(1773)
   Goldsmith died (1728–74)
Sheridan's *The Rivals* (1775)   Declaration of American Independence
Sheridan's *School for Scandal*
(1777)
(1776)

1780

IX. VICTORIAN TIMES

	1780

ROMANTIC

Monopoly of Drury Lane and
Covent Garden (1787)
French Revolution (1789)

Goethe's *Faust* in
Germany (1790)　　1790

Jane Austen's *Pride and Prejudice* (*c.* 1796)
Lyrical Ballads (1798)

Schiller's *Maria Stuart*　1800
in Germany (1800)

Napoleon emperor (1804)

1810

REGENCY

Prince of Wales Regent (1811)
Battle of Waterloo (1815)
Gas lighting first used in theatres (1817)

1820

Kemble died (1757–1823)
Stockton–Darlington Railway (1825)

Hugo's *Cromwell* in
France (1827)

Robertson born (1829–71)

Hugo's *Hernani* in France (1830)　1830

Reform Act (1832)
Kean died (1787–1833)
Victoria queen (1837–1901)

VICTORIAN

1840

Act to end monopoly of theatres:
Lord Chamberlain to license new plays (1843)
Ellen Terry born (1847–1928)
Auditorium darkened (1849)

1850

Limelight in use (1851)
Pinero born (1855–1934)
Wilde born (1856–1900)
Shaw born (1856–1950)

1860　*Great Expectations* (1860)

Robertson's *Caste* (1867)

American Civil War (1861–5)

1870

Ibsen's *Doll's House*
in Norway (1878)

Macready died (1793–1873)

	1880	Electric light in theatre use (1880)
Shaw's *Widowers' Houses* (1885)		
Ibsen's *Doll's House* in		
London (1889)		Antoine in Paris (1887–94)
	1890	
Pinero's *Second Mrs Tanqueray*		Free education (1891)
(1893)		Grein's Independent Theatre Company (1891)
Wilde's *Importance of Being*		London's first film show (1895)
Earnest (1895)		
Shaw's *Caesar and Cleopatra*		Moscow Arts Theatre formed (1898)
(1898)	1900	
		Victoria died (1901)
		Irving died (1905)
	1910	

X. THE PLAYS OF SHAW

1885	*Widowers' Houses*
1893	*The Philanderer*
	Mrs Warren's Profession
1894	*Arms and the Man*
	Candida
1895	*The Man of Destiny*
1896	*You Never Can Tell*
1897	*The Devil's Disciple*
1898	*Caesar and Cleopatra*
1899	*Captain Brassbound's Conversion*
1901	*Man and Superman*
1904	*John Bull's Other Island*
1905	*Major Barbara*
1906	*The Doctor's Dilemma*
1908	*Getting Married*
1909	*The Shewing-up of Blanco Posnet*
	Misalliance

1910	*Fanny's First Play*
1911	*Androcles and the Lion*
1912	*Pygmalion*
	Overruled
1916	*Heartbreak House*
1921	*Back to Methuselah*
1923	*Saint Joan*
1929	*The Apple Cart*
1932	*Too True to be Good*
1933	*On the Rocks*
	Village Wooing
1934	*The Simpleton of the Unexpected Isles*
1936	*The Millionairess*
1938	*Geneva*
1939	*In Good King Charles's Golden Days*
1949	*Buoyant Billions*

XI. THE TWENTIETH CENTURY

	1900	
EDWARDIAN		
Strindberg's *Easter* in Sweden (1901)		Edward VII king (1901–1910)
Yeats's *Cathleen ni Hoolihan* (1902)		Hollywood making films (1903)
Chekhov's *Cherry Orchard* in Russia (1904)		Gielgud born (1904)
		Dublin Abbey Theatre (1904)
Shaw's *Major Barbara* (1905)		English Stage Company at Royal Court (1904–7)
Granville-Barker's *Waste* (1906)		
Synge's *Playboy* (1907)		Olivier born (1907)
Galsworthy's *Strife* (1909)		Manchester Repertory formed (1907) and spread of repertory companies

EDWARDIAN

Strindberg's *Easter* in
Sweden (1901)
Yeats's *Cathleen ni Hoolihan* (1902)
Chekhov's *Cherry Orchard*
in Russia (1904)
Shaw's *Major Barbara* (1905)
Granville-Barker's *Waste* (1906)
Synge's *Playboy* (1907)
Galsworthy's *Strife* (1909)

1900

Edward VII king (1901–1910)
Hollywood making films (1903)
Gielgud born (1904)
Dublin Abbey Theatre (1904)
English Stage Company at Royal Court
(1904–7)

Olivier born (1907)
Manchester Repertory formed (1907) and
spread of repertory companies

GEORGIAN
Shaw's *Pygmalion* (1912)

1910

Old Vic founded (1914)
World War I (1914–18)
Women get the vote (1917)

1920

Pirandello's *Six Characters*
in Italy (1921)
Shaw's *Saint Joan* (1923)
O'Casey's *Juno and the Paycock* (1924)
O'Casey's *Plough and the Stars* (1926)
O'Casey's *Silver Tassie* (1928)

Eliot's *Waste Land* (1922)
2LO broadcasting (1922)

BBC constituted (1927)
First sound film (1929)

1930

O'Neill's *Mourning Becomes Electra*
in America (1931)

Group Theatre in New York (the
'Method') (1931–41)
Stratford Memorial Theatre opened (1932)

Priestley's *Dangerous Corner* (1932)
Eliot's *Murder in the Cathedral* (1935)

Hitler in power (1933)
Canterbury Festival (1935)
BBC Television service, Alexandra
Palace (1936)

Eliot's *Family Reunion* (1939)

World War II (1939–45)

1940

State support for the Arts (CEMA) (1940)

Brecht's *Mother Courage*
(German) (1941)
Anouilh's *Antigone* in France (1942)
Williams's *Glass Menagerie*
in America (1944)

The Arts Council formed (1946)
BBC's Third Programme begins (1946)
International Theatre Institute formed
(1948)

POST-WAR
Miller's *Death of a Salesman*
in America (1949)
Eliot's *Cocktail Party* (1949)
Fry's *Lady's Not For Burning* (1949)

1950

Fry's *Sleep of Prisoners* (1951)
Beckett's *Waiting for Godot*
in France (1952)
Thomas's *Under Milk Wood* (1954)
Osborne's *Look Back in Anger* (1956)
Pinter's *Birthday Party* (1958)

Money allotted for National Theatre
(1951)
Stratford, Ontario, Festival begins (1953)
The Television Act (ITA formed) (1954)
English Stage Company at Royal Court
(1956)

Glossary

ACTING AREA. The space on the stage suitable for acting.

ACTION. The progress of the play in terms of the actor's speech and movement.

ADAPTATION. Changing a work from one medium to another.

ALIENATION. A style of writing or playing which prevents the identification of the spectator with the character.

ALLEGORICAL. That type of drama whose true meaning is symbolized by the action. 'Spoken in another way.'

ANTI-CLIMAX. Action which lowers tension.

APRON-STAGE. An acting area which projects into the audience.

ARENA-STAGE. An acting area surrounded, or nearly surrounded, by spectators.

ASIDE. Speech delivered directly to the audience, not apparently heard by other characters.

AUDITORIUM. That part of the theatre occupied by the audience.

BATTENS. The lights hung in rows above the stage behind the proscenium arch.

BLANK VERSE. Unrhymed lines of five iambic feet.

BURLESQUE. A speech, scene or play ridiculing other drama.

BUSINESS. Action, usually with properties, devised to help an actor perform.

CAESURA. The slight pause in a line of verse.

CARICATURE. The mockery of a person or character by exaggerated imitation.

CATASTROPHE. The action at the end of a tragedy which brings about its *dénouement*.

CATHARSIS. The effect of tragedy on the spectator.

CHORUS. A group of actors singing, speaking or dancing together.

CLIMAX. Action which increases tension to a crisis.

COMEDY. Drama which usually induces thoughtful laughter.

COMIC RELIEF. Comic action introduced into tragedy.

COMMEDIA DELL'ARTE. The popular improvised farce of Italy and France in the sixteenth and seventeenth centuries.

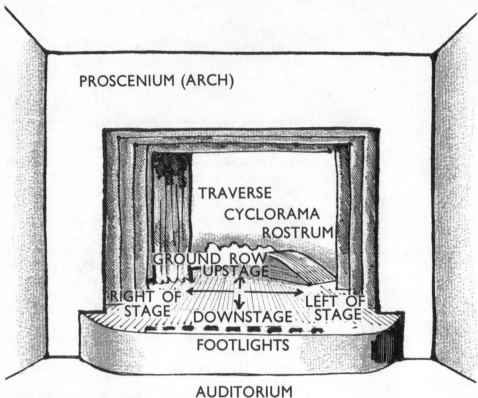

PROSCENIUM (ARCH)

TRAVERSE
CYCLORAMA
ROSTRUM

GROUND ROW
UPSTAGE

RIGHT OF
STAGE

LEFT OF
STAGE

DOWNSTAGE

FOOTLIGHTS

AUDITORIUM

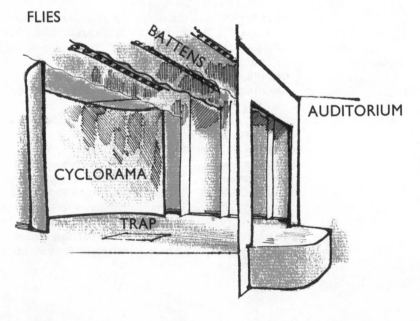

FLIES

BATTENS

AUDITORIUM

CYCLORAMA

TRAP

CONFIDANT(E). A character trusted with the hero's personal affairs.

CONVENTION. An agreement between the actor and spectator to use artificial means of creating the action.

COUPLET. A rhyming pair of lines.

CRISIS. A turning-point of tension.

CUE. The part of an actor's speech or movement when another actor must speak or move, or a signal showing when a lighting or other effect must occur.

CUTTING (film). Putting together two different shots. (A cut on television is an instantaneous change from one camera to another.)

CYCLORAMA. The blank upstage backing suitable for lighting effects.

DÉCOR. The general appearance of the setting, including the costumes.

DÉNOUEMENT. The concluding action, usually resolving the plot.

DIALOGUE. Speech between two or more actors.

DIDACTIC. Drama which teaches.

DISSOLVE (Mix). Merging one picture into another until the first has vanished (often to indicate the passage of time).

DOCUMENTARY (film). Subject or treatment taken from real life.

DOWNSTAGE. That part of the stage nearest the audience.

DUOLOGUE. Speech between two actors only.

EDITING (film). The selection of shots to be put together. *See* CUTTING.

EPIC THEATRE. Drama from Germany in the 1920s and later, consisting of a series of episodes, and often linked by narrative.

EXPOSITION. That part of a play, usually at the beginning, which tells the audience what has happened previously.

EXPRESSIONISM. A modern dramatic style expressing ideas by symbolic action and abstract characterization.

FANTASY. Drama which moves into a world of imagination or dream.

FARCE. Drama of ridiculous and improbable characters and situations.

FLIES. The tower above the stage behind the proscenium arch.

FLOODLIGHT. A movable lantern throwing undirected light (cf. Spotlight).

FOOTLIGHTS. Lights sunk in the floor downstage.

FOURTH WALL. The imaginary downstage wall of the box setting, supposedly removed to allow the audience to see the action.

GESTURE. A motion of the actor's body.

GROUNDLINGS. Those spectators in the Elizabethan theatre who stood in the yard around the platform.

GROUPING. The arrangement of actors on the stage.

HUMOUR. The quality which illuminates some aspect of human nature by comic observation.

IMPROVISING. Making drama without the help of a script.

INTERLUDE. Drama of the sixteenth century presented in the middle of other festivities.

INTONATION. The musical inflexion of the speaking voice.

IRONY. The sharing of a secret between author and spectator or character and spectator, sometimes at the expense of another character.

LEFT OF STAGE. In stage directions, the actor's left and the spectator's right.

MAKE-UP. Greasepaint on the actor's face, to help create his character under strong light.

MASK. An artificial face worn by the actor.

MASK (verb). To take a position or place a property which will hide an actor from view.

MASQUE. Spectacular and musical drama of the seventeenth century, using a mythological subject.

MELODRAMA. Popular drama of the late nineteenth century; now a play which crudely evokes the emotions.

MIME. Drama or action without words.

MIRACLE (play). Popular religious drama of the Middle Ages, showing the lives of Christ, the saints, or Old Testament figures.

MIX. *See* DISSOLVE.

MONOLOGUE. A play or a speech by one actor.

MOOD. The general feeling in the audience or on the stage.

MORALITY (play). Religious drama of the Middle Ages, symbolizing the life of man and his vices and virtues.

MOVEMENT. The changing of an actor's position on the stage.

MYSTERY (play). Popular religious drama of the Middle Ages, showing the stories of the Bible.

NATURALISM. A style of writing or playing which reproduces the speech and behaviour of real life.

OPEN STAGING. Performance without a proscenium arch.

PACE. The speed at which the action of a play proceeds.

PANNING (film). The swivelling of a stationary camera.

PARODY. The mockery of a style of writing by exaggerated imitation.

PASTORAL. Poetry or drama idealizing country life.

PATHOS. A quality in the action which induces pity in the spectator.

PAUSE. A moment of silence in the speech of a character or stillness in the action of a play.

PERSONIFICATION. Giving a human quality to an abstract idea or an inanimate object.

PITCH. The height or depth of a vocal tone.

PLOT. The story extracted from a play.

POETIC DRAMA. Drama, usually in verse, which calls on the spectator's poetic imagination.

POINTING. The actor's emphasis of a word or phrase by voice, pause or gesture.

PROBLEM PLAY. Drama raising for discussion some social or moral issue.

PRODUCER (In America, DIRECTOR). The person who directs the actors and other artists in the presentation of a play.

PROMPT BOOK. The book in which the text of a play and the details of its performance are recorded.

PROPAGANDA PLAY. Drama which tries to persuade the audience to accept the views of the author.

PROPERTY. An article on the stage to help the action of the play.

PROSCENIUM (ARCH). The frame which surrounds the modern stage and hides its mechanics.

PROTAGONIST. Now, the leading character in a play.

REALISM. Truth to life in a play's ultimate intention; opposite of romanticism.

REPRESENTATIVE. Of a character, standing for common human qualities in mankind as a whole.

RHETORIC. Extravagant and impressive speech.

RIGHT OF STAGE. In stage directions, the actor's right and the spectator's left.

RITUAL. A conventional and ceremonial pattern.

ROSTRUM. A movable platform used to build another level in a stage setting.

SATIRE. Writing which tries to correct manners or morals by ridicule.

SCENARIO (film). The working outline of shots in a film.

SENTIMENTALITY. The excessive indulgence of an emotion.

SETTING. The decorative or representational background for a scene.

SIGHT LINES. The imaginary lines in a theatre outside which the spectator cannot see the action.

SITUATION. A dramatic arrangement of an event, usually involving a relationship between two or more characters.

SOLILOQUY. A speech by an actor alone on the stage.

SPOTLIGHT. A lantern which throws directed light.

STYLIZATION. A manner of speaking or acting which exaggerates normal speech or behaviour.

SUBPLOT. A story extracted from a play subsidiary to the main one.

SYMBOLISM. A method of making a character or an action, a situation or a setting, stand for more than itself.

TEMPO. The variations in pace in which a scene is acted.

THEATRE-IN-THE-ROUND. A form of theatre in which the actors are surrounded by the spectators.

THEME. The general idea behind, or the real subject of, a play.

TIMING. The precision in time of an actor's speech, gesture or movement.

TRACKING (film). Movement of a camera on wheels or rails.

TRAGEDY. Drama which may induce pity and fear.

TRAGICOMEDY. Drama which combines the effects of tragedy and comedy.

TRAP. An opening in the floor of the stage.

TRAVERSE. A curtain which can be drawn from side to side across the stage.

TYPE. Of a character, standing for one aspect of man's nature.

UNITY OF ACTION. Action having one plot only.

UNITY OF PLACE. Action supposedly in one place only.

UNITY OF TIME. Action supposedly lasting no more than one day.

UPSTAGE. That part of the stage farthest from the audience.

VERSE DRAMA. Drama written in verse.

WELL-MADE PLAY. That kind of play, popular in the nineteenth century and after, which keeps to rules designed to capture, sustain and satisfy interest.

Basic reading lists

* Books of special help in the stage-centred reform of drama teaching and appreciation.
† Books of special help to younger readers.

I. GENERAL REFERENCE

Gassner, J., and E. Quinn (eds.)	*The Reader's Encyclopedia of World Drama*
Hartnoll, P.	*A Concise History of the Theatre*
Hartnoll, P. (ed.)	*Oxford Companion to the Theatre*
Nagler, A. M. (ed.)	*A Source Book in Theatrical History*
Nicoll, A.	*British Drama*
	World Drama

II. DEVELOPMENT OF THE THEATRE

*Burton, E. J.	*The British Theatre*
	The Student's Guide to World Theatre
†Cleaver, J.	*The Theatre through the Ages*
*Hunt, H.	*The Live Theatre*
Marshall, N.	*The Producer and the Play*
Nicoll, A.	*The Development of the Theatre*
Southern, R.	*The Open Stage and the Modern Theatre*
	The Seven Ages of the Theatre
Ward, A. C.	*Specimens of English Dramatic Criticism*
Williams, R.	*Drama in Performance*

III. GREEK DRAMA

Aristotle	*Poetics*
*†Arnott, P. D.	*An Introduction to the Greek Theatre*
Kitto, H. D. F.	*Greek Tragedy*
Lever, K.	*The Art of Greek Comedy*

IV. ENGLISH MEDIEVAL DRAMA

Axton, R.	*European Drama of the Early Middle Ages*
Craig, H.	*English Religious Drama of the Middle Ages*

Kahrl, S. J.   *Traditions of Medieval English Drama*

Pollard, A. W.   *English Miracle Plays, Moralities and Interludes*

Rossiter, A. P.   *English Drama from Early Times to the Elizabethans*

V. ELIZABETHAN AND JACOBEAN DRAMA

Bradbrook, M. C.   *Elizabethan Stage Conditions*
The Growth and Structure of Elizabethan Comedy
Themes and Conventions of Elizabethan Tragedy

Eliot, T. S.   *Selected Essays*

Ellis-Fermor, U. M.   *The Jacobean Drama*

Ford, B. (ed.)   *The Age of Shakespeare*

VI. SHAKESPEARE

*Beckerman, B.   *Shakespeare at the Globe, 1599–1609*

Bethell, S. L.   *Shakespeare and the Popular Dramatic Tradition*

†Boas, F. S.   *An Introduction to the Reading of Shakespeare*

Bradley, A. C.   *Shakespearian Tragedy*

*Brown, J. R.   *Shakespeare's Plays in Performance*

Flatter, R.   *Shakespeare's Producing Hand*

Fluchère, H.   *Shakespeare*

*Granville-Barker, H.   *Prefaces to Shakespeare*

†Hodges, C. W.   *Shakespeare and the Players*

Knight, G. W.   *Principles of Shakespearian Production*

Muir, K. and S. Schoenbaum (eds.)   *A New Companion to Shakespeare Studies*

*Nagler, A. M.   *Shakespeare's Stage*

*Styan, J. L.   *Shakespeare's Stagecraft*

Traversi, D. A.   *An Approach to Shakespeare*

*Watkins, R.   *On Producing Shakespeare*

VII. RESTORATION DRAMA

Dobrée, B.   *Restoration Comedy*
Restoration Tragedy

Dryden   *An Essay of Dramatic Poesy*

*†Seyler, A., and Haggard, S.   *The Craft of Comedy*

Wilson, J. H.   *A Preface to Restoration Drama*

VIII. EIGHTEENTH-CENTURY DRAMA

Boas, F. S.	*Eighteenth Century Drama*
Cibber, C.	*An Apology for the Life of Mr Colley Cibber, Comedian*
Johnson	*Preface to Shakespeare*
Nettleton, G. H.	*English Drama of the Restoration and Eighteenth Century*

IX. NINETEENTH-CENTURY DRAMA

Bentley, E. R.	*Bernard Shaw*
Disher, M. W.	*Blood and Thunder : Mid-Victorian Melodrama and its Origins*
Purdom, C. B.	*A Guide to the Plays of Bernard Shaw*
MacCarthy, D.	*Shaw*
Watson, E. B.	*Sheridan to Robertson*

X. MODERN DRAMA

Bentley, E. R.	*The Modern Theatre*
Brustein, R.	*The Theatre of Revolt*
Ellis-Fermor, U. M.	*The Irish Dramatic Movement*
Esslin, M.	*The Theatre of the Absurd*
Peacock, R.	*The Poet in the Theatre*
*Styan, J. L.	*The Dark Comedy*
Williams, R.	*Drama from Ibsen to Brecht*

XI. THEORY OF DRAMA

Bentley, E. R.	*The Life of the Drama*
Clark, B. H. (ed.)	*European Theories of the Drama*
Craig, E. G.	*On the Art of the Theatre*
Eliot, T. S.	*Poetry and Drama*
Ellis-Fermor, U. M.	*The Frontiers of Drama*
Nicoll, A.	*The Theatre and Dramatic Theory*
Peacock, R.	*The Art of Drama*
Styan, J. L.	*Drama, Stage and Audience*
*Styan, J. L.	*The Elements of Drama*

XII. TRAGEDY

Henn, T. R.	*The Harvest of Tragedy*
Lucas, F. L.	*Tragedy*
Steiner, G.	*The Death of Tragedy*

XIII. COMEDY

Bergson, H.	*Laughter*
Clinton-Baddeley, V. C.	*The Burlesque Tradition*
Palmer, J.	*Comedy*
Potts, L. J.	*Comedy*

Index of Playwrights and Plays

Index of Subjects